BOOK OF
TRADITIONAL ENGLISH COOKERY

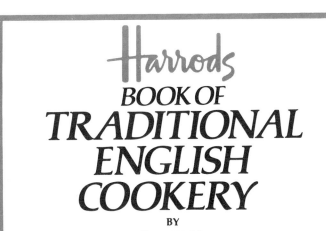

Harrods
BOOK OF
TRADITIONAL
ENGLISH
COOKERY

BY

Hilary Walden

EBURY PRESS
LONDON

Published by Ebury Press
Division of The National Magazine Company Ltd
Colquhoun House
27–37 Broadwick Street
London W1V 1FR

First Impression 1986

ISBN 0 85223 572 0

EDITORS: Fiona MacIntyre and Felicity Jackson
ART DIRECTOR: Frank Phillips
DESIGNER: Marshall Art
PHOTOGRAPHY: Grant Symon
STYLIST: Sue Russell
HOME ECONOMISTS: Susanna Tee, Janet Smith and Maxine Clark

Ebury Press would like to thank Harrods, and their archivist
Margaret Baber, for allowing the use of the black and white
illustrations taken from Harrods catalogues.

Computerset by MFK Typesetting Ltd, Hitchin, Herts
Printed and bound in Italy by New Interlitho Spa, Milan

Contents

*All eggs used in this book are size 2
unless otherwise stated.*

Introduction

TRADITIONAL English cooking has a rich and varied history, owing much of its character to the manor houses, rectories and well-to-do merchants' homes that have been the backbone of English society for so many years.

In the first century A.D., the Romans brought with them an interest in food, and a pride in developing new and unusual ways of preparing it. Cooking standards deteriorated somewhat after their departure – the success of a banquet became dependent upon the ravenous appetites of the assembled mass of diners and the sheer volume of food, rather than the quality of the food and the way it was cooked and presented.

The choice of food then was as varied as it is today, if somewhat different. Foods were natural and in many cases wild. In addition to the meats we eat today, the diet included wild boar, suckling pig, goat, kid and mutton, as well as any bird that could be shot, trapped or snared, such as bittern, curlew, peacock, lark, blackbird, thrush, rook and crow. Goats' and ewes' milk was drunk as well as cows' milk, and the sea, rivers and lakes were fully exploited for their abundant supplies of fish and shellfish.

They might not have had the exotic fruits from the tropics that line our supermarket shelves today, but our forebears picked wild berries, mulberries, quinces and medlars, and used flowers, herbs and wild produce.

The journeys of the crusaders resulted in supplies of oranges, lemons, dates, prunes and other dried fruits, almonds and the spices that are such a feature of medieval cooking. It is commonly supposed that food was heavily spiced and seasoned to diguise the taint of food that was going off, but as there was such easy access to wild food for much of the year it would have been quite unnecessary.

By Tudor and Elizabethan times, food had begun to assume much greater importance. Traders and other voyagers returned, fired with enthusiasm for the cooking they had tasted abroad, and brought back ingredients – and chefs – to recreate the dishes at their own tables. The opening of new trade routes brought different foods, not only from the East, but also from the New World – sweet potatoes from Mexico, maize, potatoes, sugars and treacle, tea, coffee and chocolate to drink.

Heavily spiced, rich foods went out of fashion under the Puritan influence of the mid-seventeenth century when pleasure in eating became unfashionable, and rich foods positively sinful. Although this severe austerity was short-lived, food generally became more simple.

The agricultural and industrial revolutions brought more changes with the emergence of a new middle class of professional men, successful traders and merchants who married into the lower nobility and aristocracy. They created new employment opportunities for the women and girls who had been driven off the land in search of work. These girls provided an abundant supply of cheap domestic labour – housemaids, kitchen-maids and cooks.

Two grades of cook soon evolved. One was the plain cook, who helped with the housework as well as providing the meals. These meals would have been very simple roasts, chops, puddings and pies, and it is from such cooks that country-style cooking began to be introduced into the diet of townspeople. The other was the 'professed' cook, employed by the higher echelons of society, who did no housework. With the help of the one or two maids she was training, she catered for the everyday meals of her master and mistress, cooked for the children in the nursery, the servants, and for the special occasion dinner parties that required more eleborate food.

Entertaining was very important to the upper middle classes and aristocracy. The lengthy, showy meals given by the wealthy were designed to impress, and people vied with each other to present their tables in the most superb fashion.

The lady of the house had to extend her repertoire of dishes, so that every space on the table could be filled. This usually meant looking to foreign sources, especially France, as French cuisine was very much in vogue. French chefs who had fled the revolution in their own country were being employed in increasing numbers by the court, nobility and aristocracy. This was the age of the great names of Louis Eustace Ude, Carème and Alexis Soyer. If a chef could not be employed full-time, one would be hired for special occasions. Those lower down the social scale would hire a cook who had been trained – or at least claimed to have been – in France. Failing all else, a perfectly normal English dish would be given a French sounding name.

By the middle of the nineteenth century, a formal dinner followed the style we still have today, with soup served first, followed by fish and then meat. The sweet pies and puddings that had been served alongside the savoury dishes joined the sweet dishes at the end of the meal.

Lunch was a less elaborate affair, consisting of something like chops or steaks, and to bridge the gap before dinner there was the new institution of afternoon tea. This coincided with the improvement in the quality of flour, a drop in the price of sugar and the development in America of an effective raising agent in 1850.

The new society of literary, political and artistic figures at that time gathered at fashionable coffee and chocolate houses or shops, then later at gentlemen's clubs, mostly in London's St James', such as the Reform Club and Boodles. Some of the best-loved traditional dishes have emanated from these establishments. Others are associated with particular fairs or festivals, such as Michaelmas Goose.

◆ REGIONAL VARIATIONS ◆

Considering the size of England, it is remarkable how varied the regional dishes are, with social class, climate, soil differences and economy of the area all affecting its food.

In the West Country of Devon and Cornwall, fish, shellfish and cream have long played an important part in the economy, and are frequent ingredients in many of the dishes of the area. In Somerset and Wiltshire, cows graze on lush pasture-land and their milk is used both for cooking and making the famous Cheddar cheese. The by-product, whey, fed the pigs which in turn provided the local products such as faggots and sausages. Traditionally, these pork specialities also had a distinct flavour from the pigs' diet of the local apples.

The fertile Vale of Evesham is renowned for its early vegetables and fruit, asparagus, strawberries and plums, though it is the country of Kent that is known as the 'garden of England', as the soil and climate are ideal for growing all manner of fruits, particularly apples, cherries and plums. It is hardly surprising that these crop up repeatedly in the local dishes.

In the midland counties of Leicestershire and Northamptonshire, pasture-lands provide not only milk and beef, but cheeses such as Stilton, which in turn have led to a thriving pig industry and local pork products such as the Melton Mowbray pork pies. The long tradition of hunting in the forests in this part of England has led to the popularity of game dishes in that region.

The generally poorer northern counties, with their harsher climate, are better known for more filling and economical fare such as pan haggerty, and for their cakes and baking. Many of the traditional recipes are cooked on a griddle or girdle as that could be heated over a peat fire – the coal needed for heating an oven being more costly.

The recipes in this book have been taken from across the whole span of history from the Middle Ages. It is often very difficult to attribute them to particular regions, as a basic recipe may be found in a number of forms in different regions, with varying stories surrounding its origin.

Much of the traditional English food is fairly simple, plain and straightforward, but it does require some practical knowledge to cook a superb roast joint; to make feather-light, crisp pastry for puddings and pies, or delicate dumplings that melt in the mouth rather than solid lumps of dough that sink to the bottom of a stew.

Even the many slow-cooked dishes found in old recipe books must be cooked in just the right way to appreciate their full flavour and see why they have withstood the test of time. Originally these dishes were cooked in large amounts in heavy casseroles or pots beside, or suspended over, the fire in an open hearth, so the liquid never boiled to toughen and shrink the fibres of the meat – they just melted and fell apart. With modern stoves, and cooking smaller quantities, it takes more care to achieve the same slow, gentle cooking of former days.

The recipes have all been adapted to suit modern tastes, ingredients and equipment, to enable the present-day cook to experience the glory of traditional English cooking easily and with confidence.

Soups and Light Dishes

THROUGHOUT history, soups have been the stand-by, sometimes even the staple diet of the poor – the poorer the person the plainer the soup. But there is a lot more to traditional English soups than meagre broths.

Inns would have large, steaming pots of soup ready to feed to travellers while they waited for their main dish of meat. In country kitchens the soup pot, full of vegetables and chunks of meat or fowl, would sit beside the fire to provide a complete meal, the well-flavoured broth often being eaten first to take the edge off the appetite.

Journeys to far-away places brought spicy soups such as mulligatawny, and by Victorian times soup had become the proper way to start a meal, especially when the soup was real turtle.

Many of the dishes that we eat today as snacks or first courses have grown up from the traditions of high tea – a meal served about six o'clock, consisting of a savoury cooked dish and cake or a cold sweet pastry. Other dishes, such as kedgeree and devilled kidneys, appeared on the breakfast tables, while others, such as angels on horseback, rounded off a formal dinner.

Almond Soup

This soup, also called white soup, dates back to medieval times when almonds were used extensively in cookery. It tastes delicate and luxurious, yet is very easy and quite economical to make.

100 g (4 oz) ground almonds	2 egg yolks
1.4 litres (2½ pints) chicken or light veal stock	salt and white pepper
	lemon juice
	25 g (1 oz) toasted flaked almonds, to serve
1 bay leaf	
150 ml (¼ pint) cream, single, double or whipping	SERVES SIX

Put the almonds into a saucepan and blend in the stock. Bring to the boil, stirring, then add the bay leaf and simmer for 30 minutes.

Remove the bay leaf, purée the soup in a blender or food processor, then return to a clean saucepan and reheat gently.

Blend the cream into the egg yolks in a bowl, then stir in a little of the soup. Pour back into the saucepan and heat gently, stirring, until the soup thickens. Do not allow to boil. Season with salt, pepper and lemon juice.

Serve the soup sprinkled with toasted almonds.

Apple Soup

Recipes for apple soups date from at least the fifteenth century, and they are especially common in the apple growing regions of Kent, Somerset and Leicestershire. This particular recipe makes a light soup that is in keeping with today's eating styles.

350 g (12 oz) Cox's
  Orange Pippin apples,
  cored and quartered
350 g (12 oz) Bramley's
  Seedling apples, cored
  and quartered
lemon juice, for
  sprinkling
200 ml (7 fl oz) medium
  dry cider
2 cinnamon sticks

3 cloves
175 ml (6 fl oz) chicken
  stock
50 ml (2 fl oz) double
  cream
50 ml (2 fl oz) soured
  cream
salt and white pepper

SERVES FOUR

Sprinkle one Bramley's Seedling quarter with lemon juice and set aside.

Put the remaining apples, cider, cinnamon and cloves in a saucepan and bring to the boil. Cover and simmer for about 10 minutes until the apples are tender.

Remove the cinnamon and cloves, then purée the apples with the stock and creams. Reheat the soup gently, stirring, but do not allow to boil. Season.

Cut the reserved apple quarter into fine strips. Serve the soup garnished with the apple strips.

Mulligatawny Soup

This soup is of Indian origin and came into the English kitchen via the members of the army and colonial service during the nineteenth century. There are many versions of the recipe but they all have a spicy curry flavour.

50 g (2 oz) butter
1.2 kg (2½ lb) chicken,
  jointed or 6 small
  chicken joints
1 onion, chopped
1 carrot, chopped
1 small turnip, chopped
about 15 ml (1 tbsp) curry
  powder
900 ml (1½ pints) white or
  brown veal stock
4 cloves

6 black peppercorns,
  lightly crushed
about 15 ml (1 tbsp)
  lemon juice
salt and pepper
30 ml (2 tbsp) cream
  (optional)
cooked rice and grated
  apple tossed in lemon
  juice, to serve

SERVES SIX

Melt the butter in a large saucepan, add the chicken and cook until a light even brown. Remove with a slotted spoon.

Stir the onion, carrot and turnip into the pan and cook, stirring occasionally, until lightly coloured. Stir the curry powder into the vegetables and cook for 1–2 minutes. Return the chicken to the pan, stir in the stock and spices and bring just to the boil. Cover and simmer very gently for about 1¼ hours.

Lift out the chicken, discard the skin and chop the flesh. Purée the liquid and return to the rinsed out pan with the chicken. Add lemon juice and seasoning to taste, then reheat. Swirl the cream into the soup as it is served and accompany with individual bowls of cooked rice and grated apple.

Potted Shrimps

The quality of the shrimps from the Lancashire town of Morecambe has been renowned since the eighteenth century. Before the days of refrigeration, they were sealed in butter in pots to preserve them.

225 g (8 oz) shelled shrimps
100 g (4 oz) unsalted butter, cubed
pinch of ground mace
salt and cayenne pepper
75–100 g (3–4 oz) cubed butter, melted

parsley sprigs, to garnish
thin slices of brown bread and lemon wedges, to serve

SERVES FOUR

Chop a quarter of the shrimps. Melt the unsalted butter slowly, carefully skimming off any foam that rises to the surface. Stir in all the shrimps and heat gently without boiling.

Remove from the heat and stir in the mace, cayenne and a little salt. Pour into pots and leave until cold, then seal. Meanwhile, let the melted butter stand until the sediment has sunk to the bottom, then gently pour off the fat, straining it through muslin. When the potted shrimps are cold seal the surface with a layer of the clarified butter dividing it equally between the pots.

Allow to set, then cover with clingfilm and keep in the refrigerator.

Leave the potted shrimps at room temperature about an hour before serving.

Garnish each pot with a parsley sprig and serve with thin slices of brown bread and butter and wedges of lemon.

Angels on Horseback

This was a popular savoury in Victorian times when oysters were plentiful and cheap. Scallops or prunes can be used in place of oysters to make archangels or devils on horseback.

8 oysters
4 bacon slices, rinded
4 slices of toast
butter, for spreading

watercress, to garnish

MAKES EIGHT

Scrub the oysters with a scrubbing brush. Hold each one in a cloth in the palm of one hand, flat-side uppermost, and prise open the shells at the hinge. Remove the oysters from their shells.

Cut each slice of bacon in half and stretch each piece with the back of a knife. Wrap a piece of bacon around each oyster and place on a grill rack with the loose ends underneath. Place under a hot grill until crisp, then turn the rolls over to crisp the underside.

Cut two circles from each slice of toast and butter the circles. Place one bacon roll on each circle of toast. Garnish with a little watercress.

ALMOND SOUP (page 10)

Bacon Froise

Froise or fraize has been mentioned in cookery recipes from the fifteenth century onwards and probably originally referred to the cooking of a batter-like mixture in the hot fat that had dripped from a joint as it cooked on a spit.

50 g (2 oz) plain flour	25 g (1 oz) unsalted butter
pepper	fried wild mushrooms or
1 egg, beaten	grilled cultivated ones
150 ml (¼ pint) milk	and tomatoes, to serve
4 slices bacon, rinded and	
cut into strips	SERVES FOUR
1 egg white	

Sift the flour into a bowl, season with pepper and form a well in the centre. Pour the egg into the well and gradually draw in the dry ingredients then beat in the milk, a little at a time, to give a smooth batter. Leave to stand for at least an hour.

Gently cook the bacon in a non-stick frying pan until the fat runs and the bacon is crisp. Drain on absorbent kitchen paper.

Whisk the egg white until stiff, but not dry and lightly fold into the batter.

Melt the butter in the frying pan then, when sizzling, add half the batter and spread out to cover the base of the pan. Cook over a moderate heat until the bottom is a light golden brown and the top is just set. Scatter the bacon over the surface of the batter and cover with the remaining batter. Cook until the top is set, then turn the 'cake' over and brown the other side.

Transfer to a warmed plate and cut into wedges. Serve accompanied by mushrooms and tomatoes.

Fricassée of Eggs

A pretty early eighteenth century luncheon dish that could also nowadays be served for supper.

6 eggs, at room	4 cooked artichoke
temperature	bottoms, sliced
90 g (3½ oz) butter	salt and pepper
45 ml (3 tbsp) plain flour	parsley sprigs or finely
350 ml (12 fl oz) veal or	chopped fresh parsley,
chicken stock	to garnish
5 ml (1 tsp) finely	crisp fried bread
chopped fresh parsley	croûtons, to serve
5 ml (1 tsp) finely	(optional)
chopped fresh thyme	
	SERVES FOUR

Simmer the eggs for 8 minutes until they are just hard-boiled. Place immediately in cold water, then remove the shells and cut four of the eggs into quarters. Place in a serving dish.

Slice the other two eggs into halves and carefully ease out the yolks. Sieve 1½ of the yolks and chop 1½ of the whites. Cut the remaining halves into half and add to the serving dish.

Melt 40 g (1½ oz) butter in a saucepan, stir in the flour and cook for 2 minutes, stirring occasionally. Gradually stir in the stock and bring to the boil, stirring. Add the herbs and simmer for 10 minutes.

Meanwhile, melt 25 g (1 oz) of the butter in a frying pan, add the artichoke slices and heat through. Add to the sauce and season well. Over a low heat, stir in the remaining butter.

Pour the sauce over the eggs. Garnish neatly with sieved egg yolk, chopped white and parsley. Arrange croûtons around the edge of the dish, if liked, and serve immediately.

Potted Beef

Potting is a very old method of preserving whereby cooked meat or fish is hermetically sealed in butter. Potted meats are delicious for first courses, picnics or packed meals. If the sealing layer of butter is unbroken and the tops of the pots remain covered, the potted beef can be kept in the refrigerator for 2–3 weeks. Leave at room temperature for 30 minutes before serving.

450 g (1 lb) lean topside of beef, cut into 2.5 cm (1 inch) cubes
350 ml (12 fl oz) dry white wine
75 ml (3 fl oz) dry Madeira
225 ml (8 fl oz) brown stock, preferably veal
2 cloves
blade of mace

6 black peppercorns, lightly crushed
3 juniper berries, crushed
1 bay leaf
salt
30 ml (2 tbsp) brandy
175 g (6 oz) unsalted butter, softened

SERVES FOUR TO SIX

Place the beef in a shallow ovenproof casserole. Add the wine, Madeira, stock, spices, bay leaf and salt. Cover tightly and cook at 130°C (250°F) mark ½ for about 2¼ hours until very tender.

Remove the meat with a slotted spoon and leave to drain. Strain the cooking liquor, then boil until reduced to 45 ml (3 tbsp).

Pound the meat to a paste, then work in the reduced liquor, the brandy and 50 g (2 oz) butter.

Pack firmly into two earthenware or glass pots, making sure there are no air pockets. Gently melt the remaining butter. Skim off the foam from the surface, then spoon the clear butter over the surface of the meat, leaving the milky residue in the pan. Leave to set, then cover and leave overnight.

Scotch Woodcock

Scotch woodcock was popular in Victorian and Edwardian England as a savoury course at the end of dinner. Nowadays, it can be served as a light first course or a tasty snack.

6 slices of bread
50 g (2 oz) unsalted butter
4 egg yolks
300 ml (½ pint) single cream
pepper and cayenne pepper
Gentleman's Relish or anchovy paste, for spreading

6 anchovy fillets, split in half lengthways and soaked in a little milk, then drained
parsley sprigs, to garnish

SERVES SIX

Toast the bread. Meanwhile, melt the butter in a heavy-based saucepan over a low heat.

Blend the egg yolks with the cream, stir into the butter and heat gently, stirring with a wooden spoon until the mixture just begins to thicken. It will continue to cook after it has been removed from the heat. Do not allow to boil. Season with black pepper and cayenne pepper.

Cut a large circle from each slice of toast and spread with Gentleman's Relish or anchovy paste. Divide the cream mixture between the toast circles. Lay two pieces of anchovy on each serving and garnish with parsley.

Kedgeree

This traditional breakfast dish has been popular since Victorian times. It has its origins in the Indian rice and lentil dish, Khichri, so it sometimes contains a little curry powder. Traditionally made from smoked haddock, kedgeree is even more delicious when made with cooked salmon.

100 g (4 oz) long grain
  rice
salt
30 ml (2 tbsp) lemon juice
150 ml (5 fl oz) single or
  soured cream
450 g (1 lb) cooked
  salmon, flaked
pinch of cayenne pepper
pinch of grated nutmeg
pepper

2 large eggs, hard-boiled
50 g (2 oz) butter
30 ml (2 tbsp) chopped
  fresh parsley
triangles of toast and
  parsley sprigs, to
  garnish

SERVES FOUR

Put the rice in a saucepan with twice its volume of boiling, salted water and simmer for 15–20 minutes, until tender and the water has been absorbed. Remove from the heat and add the lemon juice, cream, salmon and seasonings.

Peel and chop the eggs and lightly mix into the rice. Turn the mixture into a buttered ovenproof dish, dot with the butter and bake at 180°C (350°F) mark 4 for 30 minutes.

Stir in the chopped parsley. Arrange triangles of toast around the edge of the dish and garnish with sprigs of parsley.

Gloucester Cheese and Ale

This tasty recipe has been served as a farmhouse supper dish since the Middle Ages. It also used to be served in inns, with plenty of ale, when the poultry, meat or game were finished.

225 g (8 oz) Gloucester
  cheese, thinly sliced
5 ml (1 tsp) prepared
  English mustard
about 120 ml (4½ fl oz)
  brown ale

4 thick slices of
  wholemeal bread
45 ml (3 tbsp) brown ale,
  to serve

MAKES FOUR SLICES

Arrange the cheese slices in the bottom of a large shallow ovenproof dish and spread the mustard over the top.

Pour in enough brown ale to just cover the cheese. Cover with aluminium foil, then cook at 190°C (375°F) mark 5 for about 10 minutes until the cheese has softened.

Meanwhile, toast the bread and remove the crusts. Gently warm 45 ml (3 tbsp) brown ale. Sprinkle the warm ale over the toast and cover with melted cheese. Serve immediately.

FRICASSÉE OF EGGS (page 14) AND KEDGEREE (above)

Devilled Kidneys

This dish was very popular with the Edwardians especially for breakfast. Try to mix the sauce ingredients together in advance to allow their flavours to mingle and mature.

10 ml (2 tsp) Worcestershire sauce	salt and pepper
15 ml (1 tbsp) tomato purée	25 g (1 oz) unsalted butter
15 ml (1 tbsp) lemon juice	8 lamb's kidneys, skinned, halved, cores removed
15 ml (1 tbsp) prepared English mustard	15 ml (1 tbsp) chopped fresh parsley, to garnish
pinch of cayenne pepper	

Blend the first six ingredients together in a bowl to make a sauce.

Melt the butter in a frying pan, add the halved kidneys and cook them over medium heat for about 3 minutes on each side.

Pour the sauce over the kidneys and quickly stir to coat them evenly. Serve immediately, sprinkled with chopped fresh parsley.

Mock Crab

Not all Victorian cooking was rich or elaborate, – this simple cheese dish would have been served at luncheon. Nowadays, it makes an ideal snack or supper dish.

1 hard-boiled egg yolk, sieved	15 g (½ oz) cooked chicken breast, finely chopped and shredded
15 ml (1 tbsp) softened butter	lettuce leaves, sliced tomato and cucumber and thinly sliced brown bread and butter, to serve
7.5 ml (1½ tsp) prepared English mustard	
few drops anchovy essence	
pepper	
100 g (4 oz) red Leicester cheese, grated	SERVES TWO OR THREE

Reserve a little of the egg yolk and mix the remainder with the butter, mustard, anchovy essence and pepper. Mix in the cheese with a fork so that it is evenly blended but as many shreds as possible of the cheese remain separate.

Mix in the chicken lightly, then taste and adjust the seasoning if necessary. Cover and leave in a cool place for at least 2 hours for the flavours to develop.

Serve on a small bed of lettuce, in crab shells if available, garnished with the reserved egg yolk and a little sliced tomato and cucumber. Serve thinly sliced brown bread and butter separately.

Fish and Shellfish Dishes

IT IS only in comparatively recent times that the popularity and consumption of fish and shellfish have fallen, for not only does England have an extensive coastline with easy access to rich sea fishing grounds but it also has many rivers, streams and lakes that can supply an abundant quantity and diversity of first class fresh water fish to suit all tastes.

Until the sixteenth century and the Reformation the eating of fish on Fridays and other designated holy days was obligatory on religious grounds. After that, the State joined in and passed laws stating that fish only and not meat, should be eaten on Saturdays as well as Fridays – there was even an attempt to make Wednesday a fish only day as well – to stimulate the fishing industry and in turn the ship-building industry and thus – with these industries flourishing – maintain England's prestige as a seafaring nation.

Because of its perishability and transport problems only those living near to the coast were ever able to taste fresh sea fish. The only experience inland dwellers had of such fish as cod and haddock were of the dried or salted fairly non-perishable products. These were cheap, plentiful, and often of poor quality, and they therefore became a food of the poor. Fresh water fish, however, was widely available. Potting as a means of preservation was more expensive than drying or salting so was reserved for luxury foods, such as shrimps, to provide the more well-to-do living away from the coast with shellfish and the finer type of sea fish, such as sole.

With the introduction of the railways in the nineteenth century, the development of refrigeration techniques and the use of the first steam trawlers the movement of fresh fish around the country improved and for the first time many people were able to taste the true flavour of sea fish and shellfish.

Fish Cakes

Fish cakes have been a popular, quick dish since Victorian times. The type of cooked fish used can be varied according to what is available. More elaborate recipes also include a thick white sauce, which makes the cakes more like croquettes.

225 g (8 oz) potatoes, cooked	1–2 eggs, beaten
50 g (2 oz) butter	45 ml (3 tbsp) seasoned flour
350 g (12 oz) salmon, cooked and flaked	50 g (2 oz) dried breadcrumbs
15 ml (1 tbsp) finely chopped fresh thyme	vegetable oil, for frying watercress sprigs and lemon slices, to garnish
squeeze of lemon juice	
salt and pepper	
cayenne pepper	SERVES FOUR

Purée the potatoes or mash them well. Put into a saucepan, preferably non-stick, and heat gently, stirring, to dry them out completely. Beat in the butter with a wooden spoon.

Remove the pan from the heat and beat in the salmon, thyme, lemon juice and seasonings, and just enough egg to bind together. Leave to cool, then cover and chill.

Divide into four or eight portions, then, with floured hands, shape each portion into a flat cake. Coat in seasoned flour then the remaining egg, then the breadcrumbs.

Heat the oil in a frying pan, add the fish cakes and fry, turning once, until crisp and golden.

Drain on absorbent kitchen paper. Serve garnished with watercress and lemon slices.

Oyster Loaf

Now an expensive, luxury dish, this recipe dates from the time when oysters were cheap and plentiful. More economical modern versions can be made using mussels, or lightly cooked small scallops or clams, with a little fish stock in place of the oyster liquor.

1 miniature brioche, baby cottage loaf or other small roll	30 ml (2 tbsp) double cream
	cayenne pepper and white pepper
40 g (1½ oz) melted unsalted butter	finely grated lemon rind and parsley sprig, to garnish
3 large oysters	
30 ml (2 tbsp) soured cream	
	SERVES ONE

Remove the top knob from the brioche, loaf or roll. Carefully scoop out all the inside, leaving just a wall of crust and taking care not to pierce the crust. Brush the crust shell, inside and out, with melted butter, place on a baking sheet and bake at 220°C (425°F) mark 7 for 10 minutes.

Meanwhile, scrub the oysters then, holding each one in a cloth, flat side uppermost, prise open the shells at the hinge. Loosen the oysters, reserving their liquor. Add the liquor to the remaining melted butter in a saucepan, bring to the boil and boil for a few minutes to reduce the liquid.

Stir in the creams and boil until reduced to a sauce-like consistency, whisking with a small wire whisk. Season with cayenne and white pepper.

Put the oysters into the crust shells and spoon the sauce over. Garnish with lemon rind and parsley.

Fish and Chips

Fish and chips eaten out of newspaper have been such a popular English dish for over a hundred years that they have almost become an institution. Serve sprinkled with salt and pepper and accompanied by vinegar. The traditional fish batter does not contain egg, but is nevertheless light and crisp.

550 g (1¼ lb) potatoes, cut into sticks 0.3 cm (⅛ inch) square by 7.5 cm (3 in) long	*Batter*
	100 g (4 oz) self raising flour
vegetable oil, for deep frying	2.5 ml (½ tsp) baking powder
8 fillets of plaice or pieces of white fish such as haddock or cod	5 ml (1 tsp) salt and white pepper
	150 ml (¼ pint) milk
salt and pepper	SERVES FOUR

To make the batter, sift the flour and baking powder into a bowl and season. Make a well in the centre, then gradually stir in the milk to make a smooth batter. Leave to stand for 30 minutes.

Rinse the potatoes in cold water, drain thoroughly, then dry well on absorbent kitchen paper or a tea towel.

Heat the oil in a deep-fat fryer to 185°C (360°F). Fill the basket about half-full with potatoes, then gently lower into the oil. Cook until the chips are a very light golden brown, shaking the basket occasionally to prevent the chips sticking together. Drain the chips well, then spread on a baking sheet lined with absorbent kitchen paper and place in a warm oven. Cook the remaining potatoes in the same way.

Keep the oil at 180°C (360°F). Dry the fish well, coat in the batter, and fry until golden brown and crisp. Remove with a slotted spoon and drain on absorbent kitchen paper.

Increase the temperature to 195°C (390°F), add the chips and fry briefly to crisp them up. Drain on absorbent kitchen paper and season.

Herrings with Mustard Sauce

The piquancy of the sauce in this Cornish dish is a perfect foil to the richness of the herrings.

4 herrings, cleaned, heads removed	30 ml (2 tbsp) soured cream
salt and pepper	salt and white pepper
lemon juice, to taste	a selection of large capers, silverskin onions and gherkins cut into fan shapes, to serve
Sauce	
10 ml (2 tsp) mustard powder	
2 egg yolks	
50 g (2 oz) butter, diced	SERVES FOUR

Season the herrings inside and out with salt, pepper and lemon juice. Grill for 3–5 minutes on each side.

Meanwhile, prepare the sauce. Blend the mustard with the egg yolks in a bowl, then place over a saucepan of hot water and whisk until creamy.

Gradually whisk in the butter until it has all been incorporated and the sauce is thick. Remove from the heat and whisk in the cream. Season.

Place the herrings on warmed serving plates, spoon the sauce to one side of the fish. Serve with a selection of large capers, silverskin onions and gherkins cut into fan shapes.

Fish Pies

Recipes for fish pies abound as they are a useful way of using up cooked fish. Any fish can be used, although cod and haddock feature most frequently. The covering can be potato, shortcrust, flaky or puff pastry, or, as in this more unusual recipe, choux pastry.

25 g (1 oz) butter
1 shallot, finely chopped
white part of 1 long, thin
    leek, finely sliced
50 g (2 oz) mushrooms,
    diced
45 ml (3 tbsp) plain flour
300 ml (½ pint) milk
450 g (1 lb) cooked white
    fish, flaked
50 g (2 oz) peeled prawns
50 g (2 oz) shelled
    mussels
salt and pepper

cayenne pepper
lemon juice, to taste

Topping
75 g (3 oz) plain flour
50 g (2 oz) butter, diced
150 ml (¼ pint) water
2 eggs, beaten
5 ml (1 tsp) mixed dried
    herbs
salt and pepper

SERVES SIX

Melt the butter, add the shallot and leek and cook over a medium heat, stirring occasionally, until softened. Stir in the mushrooms and cook the vegetables for 2–3 minutes.

Stir in the flour and cook for 2 minutes. Gradually stir in the milk, then bring to the boil, stirring, and simmer for 5 minutes, stirring occasionally. Remove from the heat and stir in the fish, prawns, mussels, seasonings and lemon juice.

Spoon the mixture into six buttered 8.5 cm (3½ inch) ovenproof dishes.

Sift the flour for the topping on to a sheet of greaseproof paper. Put the butter and water into a saucepan and heat until the butter has melted, then bring to the boil and immediately pour in all the flour. Remove the pan from the heat and beat until it is smooth and leaves the sides of the pan. Cool slightly, then gradually beat in the eggs, beating well after each addition. Add the seasonings and mixed dried herbs.

Spoon the paste into a piping bag and pipe small bun shapes over the top of each of the dishes. Bake at 220°C (425°F) mark 7 for about 20 minutes, then reduce the temperature to 190°C (375°F) mark 4 and continue cooking until the choux pastry topping is cooked in the centre.

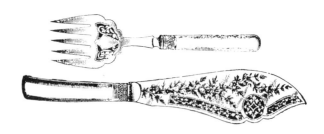

Fish Pudding

This light, moist pudding can be made with any type of cooked fish or combination of fish or shellfish. Use a melon baller to make the cucumber balls.

300 ml (½ pint) milk or single or whipping cream	5 ml (1 tsp) anchovy essence
2 bay leaves	45 ml (3 tbsp) snipped chives
25 g (1 oz) fresh breadcrumbs	salt and pepper
3 egg yolks, beaten	lemon juice, to taste
350 g (12 oz) fish, cooked and flaked	prawns, chervil sprigs and steamed cucumber balls, to garnish
100 g (4 oz) peeled prawns, chopped	

SERVES FOUR

Put the milk or cream and the bay leaves in a small saucepan and heat gently to simmering point. Pour over the breadcrumbs in a bowl and leave to soak for 10 minutes.

Remove the bay leaves, then beat in the egg yolks. Stir in the fish, prawns, anchovy essence and chives. Season with a very little salt, pepper and lemon juice. Pour into a buttered 900 ml (1½ pint) pudding basin or mould. Cover with greaseproof paper, stand in a deep baking tin and add enough boiling water to come halfway up the sides of the basin or mould. Cook at 180°C (350°F) mark 4 for about 1 hour 10 minutes until just set.

Remove the basin or mould from the heat and leave to stand for about 2 minutes before unmoulding. Garnish with prawns, chervil sprigs and steamed cucumber balls.

Water-Souchy

The name of this light fish stew (which can also be spelt water sootje) is a corruption of the Dutch waterzootje, and it reflects the strong links that existed between England and the Netherlands from Tudor times. Water-souchy is a simple fish stew that depends on the quality and freshness of the fish, the flavour of the stock and the delicacy of the cooking for success. Any combination of fish can be used, grand or humble, to suit the pocket or occasion.

50 g (2 oz) butter	900 g (2 lb) mixed fish, eg carp, perch, trout, mackerel, mullet, prepared and cut into 2.5 cm (1 inch) pieces
875 ml (32 fl oz) good fish stock	
white part of 1 thin leek, chopped	sea salt and white pepper
1 celery stick, chopped	finely chopped fresh parsley, to garnish
1 small carrot, finely chopped	
bouquet garni of 1 bay leaf, 3 chervil sprigs and 2 parsley stalks	

SERVES FOUR

Melt the butter in a saucepan, add 45 ml (3 tbsp) of the stock and the vegetables. Cover and cook over a low heat, shaking the saucepan occasionally, for 5–7 minutes until the carrot is almost tender.

Add the remaining stock and the bouquet garni and bring to the boil. Reduce the heat so the liquid just simmers and add the fish. Cook with the liquid barely moving for about 5 minutes until the fish is just tender. Season and remove the bouquet garni.

Serve sprinkled with plenty of finely chopped fresh parsley.

Dressed Crab

With its elegant simplicity, this is one of the best ways of serving top class crabs.

1 uncooked crab, about
  900 g (2 lb)
3 parsley stalks
1 bay leaf
small sprig of thyme
salt and 5 white
  peppercorns, crushed
15 ml (1 tbsp) white wine
  vinegar
30 ml (2 tbsp) fresh
  brown breadcrumbs
10 ml (2 tsp) lemon juice
white pepper

15 ml (1 tbsp) mayonnaise
  (optional)
1 egg, hard-boiled
10 ml (2 tsp) finely
  chopped fresh parsley
paprika
lettuce leaves, hard-
  boiled egg slices
  (optional) and
  cucumber twists, to
  garnish

SERVES FOUR

Place the crab in a large saucepan with the herbs, salt, peppercorns and vinegar. Cover with cold water and bring very slowly to the boil, then cover and simmer for 20 minutes. Cool in the water.

Place the crab on its back on a board with the tail flap towards you. Twist off the legs and claws close to the body, then remove the body. Discard the greyish-white gills attached to the body and the stomach bag, plus any greenish shell matter.

Carefully scrape the brown meat from the shell into a bowl using the handle of a teaspoon to get right under the shell. Scrape the pinkish curd into the bowl. Crack the claws and legs using a hammer or heavy weight and remove as much white meat as possible. Place in a separate bowl.

Tap around the shell to the natural dark line to neaten it, then scrub the shell, dry it well and rub lightly with oil to make it shine.

Mix the breadcrumbs, 5 ml (1 tsp) of the lemon juice and seasoning into the brown meat, then pack neatly into the centre of the shell, leaving room on either side for the white meat.

Season the white meat and stir in the remaining lemon juice and the mayonnaise, if using. Arrange the white meat in the sides of the shell.

Separate the yolk and white of the egg. Chop the white finely and sieve the yolk. Sprinkle a straight line of egg yolk along the lines where the white meat meets the brown. Sprinkle a row of parsley next to the two rows of yolk then a row of egg white next to the parsley rows. Sprinkle paprika in diagonal lines over the white meat to make a diamond pattern.

Place the shell on a small bed of shredded lettuce and garnish the lettuce with halved hard-boiled egg slices, if liked, and cucumber twists.

DRESSED CRAB (above)

Soles in Coffins

*A delicious Victorian luncheon dish with a
tongue-in-cheek play on the word sole (soul) in
the title. It is not as complicated as it may at
first seem as it is no more than a series of
simple steps that can be prepared separately.*

4 large potatoes	100 g (4 oz) mushrooms,
8 small sole fillets,	sliced
skinned	100 g (4 oz) peeled
salt and white pepper	prawns
2 shallots, finely chopped	parsley sprigs or peas, to
200 ml (7 fl oz) dry white	garnish
wine	baked small tomatoes, to
150 g (5 oz) butter, diced	serve
50 g (2 oz) plain flour	
300 ml (½ pint) milk	SERVES FOUR
pinch of ground mace	

Bake the potatoes at 200°C (400°F) mark 6 for about
1½ hours until soft.

Season the fillets, then roll them up skinned side
inwards. Scatter the shallots over the bottom of a
heavy frying pan or shallow flameproof casserole
that is just large enough to hold the fish. Place the
rolls on the shallots, pour the wine over, cover with
greaseproof paper and poach for 4–5 minutes until
they just flake – it is important not to overcook
them. Carefully remove the rolls from the pan.

Melt 50 g (2 oz) of the butter in a saucepan, stir in
the flour and cook gently for 2 minutes, stirring.
Remove from the heat and gradually stir in 225 ml
(8 fl oz) of the milk, then strain in the fish cooking
liquor. Bring to the boil, stirring, then simmer for
2 minutes. Add the mace and seasoning and remove
from the heat.

Cut a slice from each potato then, using a
teaspoon, carefully scoop out the centre and reserve.

Melt 25 g (1 oz) of the remaining butter, add the
mushrooms and cook for 2 minutes. Stir in the
prawns and cook for 1 minute, stirring occasionally.
Divide the sauce between the potatoes. Place two
rolls of sole in each potato, add the mushrooms and
prawns and replace the slices of potato.

Place the potatoes on a baking sheet and bake at
180°C (350°F) mark 4 for 10 minutes. Meanwhile,
mash the reserved potato flesh with the remaining
butter and milk. Season well.

Arrange the mashed potato around the edge of a
large warmed serving plate and garnish with parsley
or peas. Place the baked potatoes in the centre.
Serve with baked small tomatoes.

Salmon with Fennel Sauce

In the past, salmon was plentiful in English rivers such as the Wye, Severn and Thames. Over-fishing and pollution decreased numbers but now, as a result of controlled fishing and cleaner waters, wild English salmon is beginning to be seen once again in the shops.

4 salmon steaks, about 175 g (6 oz) each	2 egg yolks
2 shallots, chopped	100 g (4 oz) unsalted butter, softened
1 fennel bulb, quartered	fennel sprigs
1 bay leaf	salt and white pepper
2 parsley stalks, crushed	lemon juice, to taste
150 ml (¼ pint) dry white wine	
	SERVES FOUR

Place the salmon steaks in a shallow ovenproof dish. Scatter the shallots, fennel, bay leaf and parsley over the top. Pour in the wine, cover tightly and bake at 180°C (350°F) mark 4 for 15 minutes.

Strain off 100 ml (4 fl oz) of the cooking liquor. Turn off oven, re-cover the salmon and keep warm.

Boil the strained liquor until reduced to 15 ml (1 tbsp). Blend the egg yolks together in a bowl, then stir in the reduced liquor and work in half the butter. Place the bowl over a saucepan of hot water and whisk with a balloon whisk until the butter has melted. Gradually whisk in the remaining butter, whisking well after each addition, to make a thick, fluffy sauce. Remove the pan from the heat.

Chop enough of the fennel to give 10 ml (2 tsp), then add to the sauce with the seasoning, adding a little lemon juice if necessary.

Transfer the salmon to a warmed plate. Spoon the sauce over and garnish with remaining fennel.

Mackerel with Gooseberry Sauce

This gooseberry sauce should be sharp to complement the richness of the mackerel. Unless the fruit is particularly green and tart, sugar is unnecessary.

15 g (½ oz) unsalted butter	salt and pepper
225 g (8 oz) gooseberries, topped and tailed	lemon juice, to taste
	1 egg beaten
4 mackerel, cleaned, heads removed	SERVES FOUR

Melt the butter in a saucepan and add the gooseberries. Cover tightly and cook over a low heat, shaking the pan occasionally, until the gooseberries are tender.

Meanwhile, season the mackerel inside and out with salt, plenty of black pepper and lemon juice. Make two or three slashes with the point of a sharp knife in the skin on each side of the fish, then grill for 15–20 minutes, depending on size, turning once.

Purée the gooseberries in a blender or food processor or press through a sieve. Pour the purée into a clean pan, beat in the egg, then reheat gently, stirring. Season with salt and pepper. Place the mackerel on warmed serving plates and spoon the sauce beside the fish.

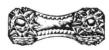

Cornish Buttered Lobster

The quality of Cornish lobsters has been famed for many years and for a magnificent dish like this such quality is essential.

2 lobsters, about 700 g (1½ lb) each, split into halves	45 ml (3 tbsp) double cream
lemon juice	salt and pepper
100 g (4 oz) butter	pinch of cayenne pepper
60 ml (4 tbsp) fresh white breadcrumbs	cucumber twists, lemon slices and dill sprigs, to garnish
45 ml (3 tbsp) brandy	

SERVES FOUR

Discard the stomach, the dark vein that runs through the body, and the spongy gills from each lobster. Remove the tail meat. Crack open the claws and remove the meat. Scrape the meat from the legs with a skewer. Cut the meat into chunks and sprinkle with lemon juice. Remove and reserve the coral, if present. Remove and reserve the soft pink flesh and liver separately.

Scrub the shells and place in a low oven to warm. Melt 50 g (2 oz) of the butter in a frying pan, add the breadcrumbs and cook until browned and crisp.

Meanwhile, melt the remaining butter in a saucepan, add the lobster flesh and stir gently until heated through.

Warm the brandy in a ladle, ignite with a taper and pour, still flaming, over the lobster. When the flames have subsided, transfer the lobster to the warmed shells using a slotted spoon and keep warm in a low oven.

Pound the liver and pink flesh. Stir into the cooking juices with the cream, a little salt and cayenne pepper and plenty of black pepper. Boil briefly until thickened, then spoon over the lobster. Sprinkle the fried breadcrumbs over the top. Quickly garnish with the reserved coral, if available, cucumber twists, lemon slices and dill sprigs.

Jugged Kippers

Kippers are herrings that have been split down the back and immersed for a short while in a very concentrated brine solution that gives the characteristic glossy sheen after drying and 4–6 hours light smoking. Originally, kippers were a pale, silvery-gold colour, but the practice of adding a dye to turn them a mahogany colour is now commonplace. For jugged kippers, try to find undyed kippers – then this simple method will show just how good kippers can be.

4 kippers	thin slices of brown bread, to serve
lemon wedges, parsley sprigs and a knob of unsalted butter (optional), to garnish	SERVES FOUR

Stand the kippers tail end up in a deep stoneware jar. Pour boiling water over the fish, but not the tails. Cover with a cloth and leave for 5 minutes.

Pour the water from the jug, then carefully remove the kippers, but not by their tails.

Serve on warmed plates with lemon wedges, parsley sprigs and a knob of unsalted butter, if wished, accompanied by slices of brown bread.

SOLE 'STEWED' IN CREAM (page 31)

Arundel Mullet

Mullet, especially the finer-fleshed red mullet, has been a favourite fish in England for hundreds of years although, like many varieties, it almost disappeared from our tables in the 1940s. Now it is making a come-back and is becoming more readily available. In this recipe, which dates from the seventeenth century, the combination of red and white wine produces a style that is more like the old 'clairet' than present day claret.

4 red mullet	salt and white pepper
150 ml (¼ pint) dry white wine	3 lemon slices, rind and pith removed
150 ml (¼ pint) light, fruity red wine	40 g (1½ oz) unsalted butter, diced
3 anchovy fillets	small thyme sprigs and snipped chives, to garnish
pinch of freshly grated nutmeg	
sprig of thyme	
1 bay leaf	SERVES FOUR

Make three slashes with the point of a sharp knife in the skin on either side of each fish. Arrange them in a single layer in a large frying pan that will just hold them comfortably, then add the wines, anchovy fillets and nutmeg and herbs.

Cover with greaseproof paper and poach gently for about 20–25 minutes until the flesh is almost tender. Lift the fish from the liquid and boil the liquid until reduced by half.

Remove the herbs, add the seasoning and lemon slices, then return the fish to the pan and cook gently for a further 5 minutes. Transfer the fish to warmed plates. Gradually whisk the butter into the sauce. Serve the fish with the sauce spooned around and garnished with small thyme sprigs and snipped chives.

Haddock and Parsley Sauce

A classic English dish that is at its best when made with really fresh haddock.

4 haddock fillets, about 175 g (6 oz) each	45 ml (3 tbsp) finely chopped fresh parsley
salt and pepper	lemon juice, to taste
100 ml (4 fl oz) milk	diced tomato flesh and flat-leaved parsley, to garnish
175 ml (6 fl oz) single cream	
175 ml (6 fl oz) fish stock	
2 small egg yolks	SERVES FOUR
25 g (1 oz) butter, diced	

Place the haddock in a shallow saucepan, season well, add the milk and cream and bring slowly to simmering point. Cover and poach for 5 minutes.

Meanwhile, put the stock in a saucepan and boil until reduced to 25 ml (1 fl oz).

Transfer the fish to a warmed shallow dish, cover and keep warm. Stir a little of the cooking liquid into the reduced stock, then blend into the egg yolks. Bring the remaining liquid to the boil, then gradually blend into the egg yolks. Return to the rinsed out pan and heat gently, stirring, until thickened. Do not allow to boil. Stir in the butter and the parsley.

Remove from the heat, season and add a little lemon juice if necessary. Divide between four warmed plates and place the fish beside the sauce. Garnish with diced tomato and flat-leaved parsley.

Sole 'Stewed' in Cream

The old name for this dish should not be taken too literally – the liquid should barely bubble and the fish only be cooked briefly.

4 sole fillets, skinned and
  cut in halves
  lengthways
25 g (1 oz) butter
15 ml (1 tbsp) finely
  chopped shallots
300 ml (½ pint) fish stock
blade of mace
225 ml (8 fl oz) double
  cream
salt and white pepper

Garnish
lobster coral or salmon
  eggs
cooked crayfish or prawns
puff pastry fleurons or
  croûtes of bread
parsley sprigs
lemon twists

SERVES FOUR

Tie each strip of sole into a loose knot in the centre. Melt half the butter in a large frying pan, add the shallot, cover and cook, shaking the pan occasionally, until softened. Stir in the stock and mace and boil rapidly until reduced to 50 ml (2 fl oz). Remove the mace.

Stir in half the cream and bring to the boil. Lower the heat, season lightly and gently lower the fish into the pan. Spoon cream over the fish. Cover with buttered greaseproof paper and poach gently for about 3 minutes until the fish just flakes.

Carefully transfer the fish to a warmed plate using a fish slice, cover and keep warm. Boil the cooking liquid until slightly thickened. Stir in the remaining butter and adjust the seasoning, if necessary.

Spoon the sauce over four warmed plates. Arrange the fish on top and garnish attractively with lobster coral or salmon eggs, crayfish or prawns, puff pastry fleurons or croûtes of bread, parsley and lemon twists.

Meat Dishes

THE ENGLISH have always enjoyed eating meat and for a long time thought that the amount of meat in the diet indicated the level of both success and prosperity. It was only the well-off who could afford ample supplies and, indeed, they would tend to eat meat, usually roasted, almost to the exclusion of all else, except game.

The less wealthy could only afford the cheaper cuts that needed slow, moist cooking to make them tender. The meat was frequently eked out with vegetables and cereals, thus developing the tasty casseroles, stews, puddings and pies that are a strong feature in English cooking.

Only the very rich and influential could afford fresh meat during the winter months. Most households had to make do with the salted, cured and potted meats that were traditionally prepared in the autumn when the breeding stock was slaughtered.

Nowadays, it is not necessary to kill off live stock with the approach of winter and modern methods of preservation and refrigeration have done away with the necessity for using salt to keep meat palatable. However, ham and bacon are still prepared in large quantities simply because they are part of the English way of eating. Sausages were a by-product of the autumnal slaughter but they, too, exist now because of their popularity not just out of necessity.

Melton Mowbray Pork Pie

*Raised pork pies are made all over England but
more especially in the hunting shire counties.
The distinguishing feature of a Melton Mowbray
pie is the inclusion of a small amount of
anchovy essence.*

900 g (2 lb) lean pork, cut
  into 0.5 cm (¼ inch)
  dice
3 bacon slices, finely
  diced
5 ml (1 tsp) finely
  chopped fresh sage
5 ml (1 tsp) finely
  chopped fresh thyme
5 ml (1 tsp) anchovy
  essence
2.5 ml (½ tsp) ground
  mace
2.5 ml (½ tsp) allspice
salt and pepper

450 ml (¾ pint) jellied
  stock
beaten egg, for glazing

Hot Water Crust Pastry
450 g (1 lb) strong plain
  flour
pinch of salt
1 egg yolk
175 g (6 oz) lard, diced
100 ml (4 fl oz) milk and
  water mixed

SERVES ABOUT EIGHT

Make the pastry, warm a mixing bowl and sieve the
flour and salt into it. Make a well in the centre and
add the egg yolk.

Gently heat the lard in the milk and water until it
has melted then bring the liquid rapidly to the boil.
Pour immediately into the well in the flour and draw
the ingredients together with a wooden spoon to
form a soft, pliable but not sticky ball of dough.

Transfer to a lightly floured surface and knead
until it is smooth and a slight resistance develops.
Cover the dough with clingfilm and leave to rest in a
warm place for 20–30 minutes.

Mix together the pork, bacon, sage, thyme,
anchovy essence, spices, a little salt and pepper.
Moisten with 45 ml (3 tbsp) of the stock.

Roll out two thirds of the pastry on a lightly
floured surface and mould around a 1.1 kg (2½ lb)
floured straight-sided jam jar, or line a raised pie
mould or drop-sided terrine. If using a jar, leave the
pastry to set on a baking sheet, then gently ease out
the jar.

Pack the meat mixture into the pastry. Roll out the
remaining pastry to make a lid for the pie. Press the
edges together tightly to seal them. Scallop the
edges and make two small holes at opposite sides or
ends of the lid and insert a funnel of foil in each. Tie
a double thickness of buttered greaseproof paper
around the outside of the pie if formed using a jam
jar. Brush the top with beaten egg. Place on a baking
sheet if using a mould or terrine.

Bake at 200°C (400°F) mark 6 for 20 minutes, then
reduce the temperature to 180°C (350°F) mark 4 and
cook for a further 2¼ hours. Remove the mould or
greaseproof paper, brush the sides and top with egg
and return to the oven for 10–15 minutes until well
browned.

Remove the pie from the oven and leave until
almost cold. Heat the stock to the consistency of egg
white. Remove the foil funnel and pour in the stock
through a funnel. Leave the pie in a cool place
overnight.

Steak, Kidney and Oyster Pudding

The meat for this dish can be cooked from raw in the pastry case, but because a longer steaming time is needed the pastry tends to become a little soggy and heavy. In this recipe the meat is cooked beforehand, and the flavour of the filling is improved by the overnight standing; surplus fat can also be removed. The addition of oysters dates from the days of Mrs. Beeton, when they were cheap. They can be replaced by additional mushrooms if wished.

25 g (1 oz) beef dripping
1 onion, chopped
750g (1½ lb) stewing
   steak, trimmed and cut
   into 2.5 cm (1 inch)
   cubes
30 ml (2 tbsp) seasoned
   flour
150 g (5 oz) lamb or ox
   kidney, trimmed and
   cut into 2.5 cm (1 inch)
   cubes
100 g (4 oz) mushrooms
425 ml (¾ pint) brown
   stock, preferably veal,
   or half stock and half
   brown ale
bouquet garni of 1 bay
   leaf, 6 parsley stalks,
   sprig of thyme

salt and pepper
1 dozen oysters (optional)

Crust
225 g (8 oz) self raising
   flour
5 ml (1 tsp) baking
   powder
5 ml (1 tsp) finely grated
   lemon rind
15 ml (1 tbsp) finely
   chopped fresh parsley
75 g (3 oz) shredded suet
50 g (2 oz) hard butter,
   finely diced
1 egg, beaten

SERVES FOUR TO SIX

The day before the pudding is required, melt half the dripping in a frying pan, add the onion and cook for 2–3 minutes.

Coat the steak in seasoned flour, then add to the pan and fry, stirring occasionally, until lightly browned. Transfer to a casserole.

Coat the kidney in seasoned flour, stir into the pan and cook for 2–3 minutes. Add to the casserole.

Melt the remaining dripping and cook the mushrooms for 2–3 minutes. Add to the casserole. Stir the stock, and brown ale if using, into the pan, dislodging the sediment, and bring to the boil. Add the bouquet garni and seasoning and pour over the meat. Stir, then cover tightly and cook at 180°C (350°F) mark 4 for 1½–2 hours. Leave, covered, in a cool place overnight.

The day of eating, stir the flour, baking powder, seasoning, lemon rind and parsley together. Stir in the suet and butter, then add the egg and sufficient water to give a soft, pliable but not sticky dough.

Knead lightly, then on a lightly floured surface, roll out to a 25 cm (10 inch) round. Cut out one quarter of the dough in a fan shape to within 2.5 cm (1 inch) of the centre.

Remove the bouquet garni and the fat from the surface of the meat. If there is an excessive amount of liquid, pour it off and boil it until reduced. (This is not so important if oysters are not usd.)

Scrub the oysters then, holding each one in a cloth, flat side uppermost, prise open the shells at the hinge. Loosen the oysters and add them, with their liquor, to the meat. Check the seasoning.

Line an 850 ml (1½ pint) pudding basin with three quarters of the pastry and fill with the meat and oyster mixture. Roll out the remaining piece of dough to a round 2.5 cm (1 inch) larger than the top of the basin. Dampen the exposed edge of the dough lining the basin. Lift the round of dough on top of the meat and oyster filling and press the pastry edges together to seal.

Cover with a circle of greaseproof paper, then a

piece of foil pleated across the centre and tied in place with string.

Put the basin in a large saucepan with enough boiling water to come halfway up the sides of the basin. Cover and steam for 1½–2 hours, topping up with boiling water if necessary. Serve the pudding in the basin with a white napkin or cloth tied around.

Leg of Lamb with Crabmeat Stuffing

This is based on an early nineteenth century recipe, the flavours of which combine extremely well without overpowering each other. The original recipe calls for a crab or lobster sauce to be served under the leg but a more practical herb-flavoured English butter sauce works as well, if not better. The dill complements both lamb and crab.

1.8 kg (4 lb) leg of young
   lamb, boned
salt and pepper
225 g (8 oz) crabmeat
25 g (1 oz) fresh
   breadcrumbs
finely grated rind of
   1 lemon
freshly grated nutmeg
pinch of cayenne pepper
1 egg yolk
1 celery stick, finely
   chopped
white part of 1 thin leek,
   finely chopped

75 ml (3 fl oz) dry white
   wine

Sauce
225 g (8 oz) unsalted
   butter, diced
25 g (1 oz) plain flour
150 ml (¼ pint) water
about 22.5 ml (1½ tbsp)
   finely chopped fresh
   dill
lemon juice, to taste
salt and white pepper

SERVES SIX

Season the lamb inside and out. Mix the crabmeat, breadcrumbs, lemon rind, nutmeg, cayenne and seasoning together. Bind lightly with egg yolk. Fill the cavity in the leg with the mixture and sew it up.

Place the celery and leek in a casserole. Season and place the lamb on top. Pour the wine over, cover and cook at 180°C (350°F) mark 4 for about 1½ hours until the lamb is almost tender.

Transfer the lamb to a rack placed in a roasting tin and return it to the oven for about 20 minutes to brown the outside.

Meanwhile, make the sauce. Melt one third of the butter. Blend the flour with the water and whisk into the melted butter using a balloon whisk. Heat to simmering point then leave over a low heat for about 20 minutes, stirring occasionally.

Gradually whisk in the remaining butter, making sure each piece is fully incorporated before adding the next. Add the dill and lemon juice to taste and season with salt and pepper.

While the sauce is cooking over a low heat, leave the lamb in a warm place for about 15 minutes.

Serve the lamb, carved into slices, accompanied by the dill and butter sauce.

Lamb Cutlets Reform

This dish was created by Alexis Soyer when he was chef at the Reform Club in Pall Mall. He poured the classic French sauce, **poivrade,** *over a garnish of hard-boiled egg white, mushrooms, truffles, tongue and gherkins and served ham and breadcrumb-coated mutton or lamb cutlets to the side accompanied by redcurrant jelly.*

12–18 lamb cutlets,
  depending on size
1 egg beaten
about 75 g (3 oz) fresh
  white breadcrumbs
20 g (¾ oz) ham, very
  finely chopped
50 g (2 oz) unsalted butter

Sauce
25 g (1 fl oz) vegetable oil
2 Spanish onions,
  chopped
2 carrots, chopped
1 celery stick, chopped
30 ml (2 tbsp) plain flour
100 ml (4 fl oz) red wine
  vinegar
450 ml (16 fl oz) dry white
  wine
4 juniper berries, lightly
  crushed

bouquet garni of
  6 parsley stalks, 1 bay
  leaf and a sprig of
  thyme
2 litres (3½ pints) brown
  stock, preferably veal
10 black peppercorns,
  lightly crushed and tied
  in muslin
salt

Garnish
white of 2 hard-boiled
  eggs
2 mushroom caps
20 g (¾ oz) tongue
1 gherkin
20 g (¾ oz) truffle
  (optional)
redcurrant jelly, to serve

SERVES SIX

First make the sauce, heat the oil in a large saucepan, add the vegetables and cook, stirring occasionally, until golden brown.

Sprinkle the flour over and cook gently, stirring frequently, until a rich golden brown. Stir in the vinegar and half the wine, dislodging any sediment, and cook gently until the liquid is reduced to a syrupy consistency.

Stir in the remaining wine, the juniper berries, bouquet garni and stock. Simmer gently, removing any scum occasionally, for about 3 hours until the sauce is well-reduced.

Pass the sauce through a conical strainer or fine sieve, pressing down well on the vegetables, then strain through muslin into a clean saucepan. Add the peppercorns and simmer for about 10 minutes. Adjust the seasoning and either boil to reduce to about 600 ml (1 pint) or add extra stock if necessary. Remove the peppercorns.

Coat the lamb cutlets in egg, allowing the excess to drain off. Mix the breadcrumbs and ham together on a flat plate. Coat the lamb cutlets evenly and lightly in the breadcrumb and ham mixture, pressing it well into the surface.

Melt three quarters of the butter in a large frying pan and cook the lamb for 3–4 minutes each side, depending upon their thickness. Fry them in batches if necessary so they are not crowded in the pan and add extra butter as necessary.

Cut the garnish ingredients into fine strips, mix together and arrange on a warmed large serving platter, leaving plenty of space for the lamb. Carefully pour the sauce over the garnish and arrange the lamb cutlets next to it. Serve the cutlets with redcurrant jelly.

LAMB CUTLETS REFORM (above)

Boiled Beef and Carrots

A classic Cockney way of cooking beef that had been preserved for the winter months by salting. Order the meat in advance and check whether it needs soaking.

1.6 kg (3½ lb) lean salted brisket or silverside of beef
bouquet garni of 1 bay leaf, 6 parsley stalks, small sprig of rosemary, sprig of thyme
6 black peppercorns, lightly crushed
2 small onions, quartered and a clove stuck in each quarter

1 carrot, quartered
2 small turnips, quartered
2 celery sticks, chopped
1 leek, chopped
12 small carrots
peas and mashed potatoes or dumplings, to serve

SERVES SIX

Place the beef in a large saucepan, add just enough water to cover and bring slowly to the boil. Remove the scum from the surface, add the bouquet garni, peppercorns, onion, carrot quarters, turnip, celery and leek. Lower the heat and simmer very gently for about 2 hours. Add the small carrots and simmer gently for a further 30–40 minutes or until the carrots are tender.

Carefully transfer the beef and small carrots to a warmed serving plate and keep warm. Strain the cooking liquor and remove the fat from the surface. Boil the liquid to reduce slightly then pour into a warmed sauceboat.

Serve the beef surrounded by the carrots, accompanied by peas and mashed potatoes or dumplings, with the sauce handed separately.

Beef Olives

The actual origin of the name of this very English of dishes is a little uncertain – it is most likely that it is so called because the shape resembles olives. It has been popular from the early 1800s and this is one of the most tasty versions.

75 g (3 oz) bacon, rinded and chopped
1 small onion, chopped
10 ml (2 tsp) finely chopped fresh parsley
100 g (4 oz) fresh breadcrumbs
50 g (2 oz) shredded suet
1.25 ml (¼ tsp) mixed dried herbs
1 lemon
1 small egg, beaten
salt and pepper
about 700 g (1½ lb) topside of beef, cut into 8 thin slices
about 15 ml (1 tbsp) prepared English mustard

2 bacon slices, rinded and chopped
2 shallots, chopped
1 carrot, chopped
1 very small turnip, chopped
300 ml (½ pint) brown stock, preferably veal
150 ml (¼ pint) red wine
50 ml (2 fl oz) Marsala
1 bay leaf
parsley sprigs, to garnish
baby carrots, baby turnips and whole shallots, to serve

SERVES FOUR

Mix the first six ingredients together, add the grated rind of half the lemon and 5 ml (1 tsp) of the juice. Bind together with the egg, then season.

Flatten each slice of beef between two sheets of damp greaseproof paper, then spread sparingly with mustard. Divide the stuffing between the slices, fold the sides over and roll up into neat parcels. Secure with fine string.

Heat the slices of bacon gently in a shallow flameproof casserole until the fat runs, then remove the bacon with a slotted spoon. Place the beef rolls in the casserole and fry over medium heat until lightly browned. Remove with a slotted spoon.

Add the shallots, carrot and turnip and fry until the shallots are beginning to soften. Stir in the stock, wine and Marsala, and bring to the boil. Return the bacon and beef rolls to the casserole, add the bay leaf and season lightly. Cover with foil and the lid and cook at 170°C (325°F) mark 3 for about 1½ hours.

Transfer the beef rolls to a warmed serving plate, remove the bay leaf from the liquid and purée the liquid. Bring to the boil and boil for a few minutes to thicken it slightly. Adjust the seasoning and pour over the beef.

Garnish with parsley sprigs and serve surrounded by baby carrots, baby turnips and whole shallots.

Pomes Dorryle

The modern name for this dish, which is basically a type of pork rissole, would be Glazed or Gilded Apples. In the medieval recipe, on which this version is based, the gilding took the form of a thick paste of flour, honey and saffron, a combination which is a little expensive and not quite to today's tastes.

450 g (1 lb) lean pork, minced
15 ml (1 tbsp) finely chopped fresh marjoram
3 sage leaves, finely chopped
2.5 ml (½ tsp) ground mace
salt and pepper
3 eggs, beaten

about 60 ml (4 tbsp) fresh white breadcrumbs
white pepper
vegetable oil for deep frying
fried apple rings or apple sauce and watercress, to serve

SERVES FOUR

Mix the pork, herbs, mace and salt and pepper together, then bind with two thirds of the beaten egg. Form the mixture into 12 small balls, place on a rack in a roasting tin and bake at 180°C (350°F) mark 4 for about 20 minutes. Leave to cool.

Mix the breadcrumbs with salt and white pepper. Coat the pork balls in the remaining egg, allowing the excess to drain off, then toss in the breadcrumbs until coated.

Heat the oil in a deep-fat fryer to 180°C (350°F). Add the pork balls and fry for 3–4 minutes until crisp and golden. Drain on absorbent kitchen paper, then serve immediately with fried apple rings or apple sauce and watercress.

Veal Collops

A collop or escalope is a thick slice of boned meat cut across the grain which is then flattened before cooking. It can be beef, venison, lamb or, as in this recipe, veal.

4 veal escalopes, about 100 g (4 oz) each, cut into halves	10 ml (2 tsp) plain flour
	salt and pepper
	pinch of ground mace
65 g (2½ oz) butter	
1 small onion, chopped	*Garnish*
175 ml (6 fl oz) dry white wine	crisp bacon rolls
	button mushroom caps
400 ml (14 fl oz) veal stock	lemon twists
5–10 ml (1–2 tsp) mushroom ketchup	parsley sprigs
about 15 ml (1 tbsp) lemon juice	SERVES FOUR

Flatten each veal escalope between two sheets of damp greaseproof paper.

Melt 50 g (2 oz) butter in a frying pan, add the veal and cook for about 2 minutes on each side. Transfer to a warmed plate and keep warm.

Add the onion to the pan and cook for about 3 minutes, stirring frequently, until softened but not browned. Stir in the wine and boil until almost evaporated. Stir in the stock, mushroom ketchup and lemon juice, bring to the boil and simmer until reduced to 225 ml (8 fl oz).

Work the flour into the remaining butter, then gradually whisk into the stock to thicken it slightly. Season with salt, pepper and mace, taste and add more mushroom ketchup and lemon juice if necessary.

Arrange the collops, overlapping each other, on a warmed oval meat platter. Spoon some of the sauce down the centre of the collops and garnish with bacon rolls, mushroom caps, lemon twists and parsley sprigs. Serve the remaining sauce separately.

Beef Hare

A tougher cut of beef when cooked slowly and spiced like this, is beautifully tender and has a flavour like hare.

900 g (2 lb) chuck steak, cut into strips about 7.5×2.5 cm (3×1 inch)	1 onion, cut into quarters and each piece stuck with 2 cloves
flour seasoned with salt, pepper and plenty of freshly grated nutmeg	1 small young parsnip, shredded
	150 ml (5 fl oz) red wine
5 ml (1 tsp) celery seeds	SERVES FOUR

Toss the meat in the seasoned flour, then pack into a deep 900 ml (1½ pint) earthenware pot, scattering celery seeds in between the layers.

Arrange the onion and parsnip on top, pour in the wine, cover tightly and leave for about 2 hours.

Place in an oven at 220°C (425°F) mark 7 and immediately reduce the temperature to 170°C (325°F) mark 3. Cook for 2¼ hours or until the beef is completely tender.

VEAL COLLOPS (above)

Spiced Beef

Spiced beef is traditional Christmas fare in Leicestershire, and parts of Yorkshire. It is ideal for a buffet at any time of the year, for picnics or packed meals. Once cooked it can be kept, well-wrapped, in the refrigerator for 1–2 weeks.

1.8 kg (4 lb) lean, boned topside or silverside of beef
100 g (4 oz) coarse sea salt
15 ml (1 tbsp) crushed juniper berries
15 ml (1 tbsp) cloves
15 ml (1 tbsp) crushed black peppercorns
15 ml (1 tbsp) whole allspice
1 blade of mace
1 bay leaf
5 ml (1 tsp) chopped fresh thyme
75 g (3 oz) dark brown sugar
7.5 ml (1½ tsp) saltpetre
150 ml (¼ pint) red wine

To serve
horseradish sauce
beetroot
thinly sliced brown bread and butter or crusty bread
pickled onions and other pickles

SERVES EIGHT TO TEN

Rub all the surfaces of the beef with the salt, roll the meat up and place it in an earthenware pot. Cover and leave in a cool place overnight.

Crush the spices and herbs together, then crush with the sugar and saltpetre. Dry the surface of the meat with absorbent kitchen paper. Tip any liquid from the pot. Rub the spice mixture all over the meat, roll it up and return it to the pot. Cover and leave in a cool place for 9 days, turning the meat daily and rubbing in the spice mixture.

Dry the beef well with absorbent kitchen paper, place it in an ovenproof earthenware pot that will just hold it comfortably and pour the wine over.

Cover tightly and cook at 170°C (325°F) mark 3 for about 3 hours or until the beef is tender.

Remove from the oven and leave in a cool place for about 3 hours. Drain the meat, place it between two boards, and put heavy weights on top. Leave in a cool place for 24 hours.

Carve into thin slices and serve with horseradish sauce, beetroot and thin brown bread and butter or crusty bread, pickled onions and other pickles.

Brown Ragoo of Lamb

The spelling of this dish, an adaptation of the French ragoût, is an example of that country's influence on English culinary matters. Peas or flageolet beans could be used in place of broad beans.

75 g (3 oz) butter, diced
900 g (2 lb) leg of lamb, cut into 2.5 cm (1 inch) pieces
750 ml (1¼ pints) brown stock, preferably veal
1 onion, unpeeled, stuck with 4 cloves
salt and pepper
3 parsley sprigs
2 thyme sprigs
2 bay leaves
small sprig of rosemary
3 carrots, cut into quarters
12 small onions
100 g (4 oz) button mushrooms
squeeze of lemon juice
75 g (3 oz) shelled broad beans, cooked, to serve
flesh of 2 large firm tomatoes, diced and
30 ml (2 tbsp) finely chopped fresh parsley, to garnish

SERVES SIX

Melt 40 g (1½ oz) of the butter in a large heavy frying pan, add the lamb in batches and cook until an even golden brown. Transfer to a casserole using a slotted spoon. Reserve the butter in the pan.

Put the stock in a saucepan with the unpeeled onion, seasoning and herbs and bring to the boil. Pour over the lamb, cover tightly and cook at 180°C (350°F) mark 4 for about 1 hour, stirring occasionally.

Meanwhile, add another 15 g (½ oz) butter to the frying pan and melt. Add the carrots and small onions and fry until lightly browned.

Drain on absorbent kitchen paper then stir into the casserole. Cover tightly again and cook for a further 30 minutes. Cook the mushrooms in the remaining butter with a squeeze of lemon juice. Drain on absorbent kitchen paper.

Remove the onion stuck with cloves from the casserole, then stir in the mushrooms and cook, uncovered, for 10 minutes. Using a slotted spoon, lift the meat and vegetables from the dish and keep warm. Boil the liquid until it is reduced to about 400 ml (14 fl oz), then pour into a warmed jug.

Arrange the meat on a large warmed serving plate with the vegetables, adding the broad beans, and pour over some sauce. Garnish with the tomato flesh and the parsley. Serve, with the rest of the sauce handed separately.

Lancashire Hot-Pot

This dish – which gets its name from the deep earthenware pot that was traditionally used – has a number of regional variations. In these, ham, mushrooms or even oysters too may be added.

6 potatoes, thinly sliced	2 onions, thinly sliced
salt and pepper	200–300 ml (7–10 fl oz)
8 best end of neck lamb	chicken stock
chops	about 25 g (1 oz) dripping
4 lamb's kidneys,	or butter, melted
skinned, halved and	
cored	SERVES FOUR

Grease a deep, earthenware ovenproof pot. Lay about one third of the potatoes in the bottom and sprinkle with salt and pepper. Pack in four of the chops, followed by two of the kidneys, then half of the onion, seasoning each layer well.

Repeat the layering, finishing with a layer of neatly overlapping potato slices. Pour in sufficient stock to half-fill the pot, then brush the potato covering with melted dripping or butter.

Cook at 220°C (425°F) mark 7 for 30 minutes, then reduce the temperature to 140°C (275°F) mark 1, cover and cook for 2 hours. Increase the heat to 200°C (400°F) mark 6, uncover the pot and cook for a further 30 minutes.

Braised Beef with Chestnuts and Celery

This well-flavoured casserole, which dates from the eighteenth century, would have been made in the late autumn and winter when both celery and fresh chestnuts were available. It could be made at any time of the year nowadays using imported celery and where necessary canned or reconstituted dried chestnuts.

18 chestnuts, fresh,
   drained canned or
   reconstituted dried
30 ml (2 tbsp) beef
   dripping
2 bacon slices, rinded and
   chopped
900 g (2 lb) stewing steak,
   cut into cubes
1 onion, chopped
15 ml (1 tbsp) plain flour
300 ml (½ pt) brown ale

300 ml (½ pint) brown
   stock, preferably veal
pinch of grated nutmeg
juice and finely grated
   rind of 1 orange
salt and pepper
3 celery sticks, chopped
finely chopped fresh
   parsley, to garnish

SERVES SIX

Slit the skins of fresh chestnuts, then cook in simmering water for about 7 minutes. Peel off the thick outer skin and thin inner skin while still warm, removing from the water one at a time.

Melt the dripping in a flameproof casserole, add the bacon and beef in batches and cook, stirring occasionally, until browned. Remove the meat with a slotted spoon and drain thoroughly on absorbent kitchen paper.

Add the onion to the casserole and fry, stirring, until softened. Drain off most of the fat and reserve. Return the meat to the casserole, sprinkle in the flour and cook, stirring, for 1–2 minutes.

Stir in the brown ale, stock, nutmeg, orange juice and half the rind and the seasoning. Bring to the boil, stir well to dislodge the sediment, then add the fresh or dried chestnuts. Cover tightly with foil and a lid and cook at 170°C (325°F) mark 3 for about 45 minutes.

Meanwhile, heat the reserved fat in a saucepan, add the celery and fry lightly. Add to the casserole after the 45 minutes cooking time, re-cover and cook for about 1 hour. (If using canned chestnuts, add them after 30 minutes, re-cover the casserole and continue cooking for the remaining 30 minutes.)

Serve with the remaining orange rind and the parsley sprinkled over the top.

BROWN RAGOO OF LAMB (page 42)

Boiled Mutton with Caper Sauce

Mutton is the flesh from a lamb that has lived passed its first birthday. It is difficult to find nowadays as it is popularly believed to be too fatty and inferior. However, it does have a good flavour and is well worth using for this recipe – excess fat can easily be trimmed. Lamb can be used as an alternative.

3 kg (5 lb) leg of mutton (or lamb)	*Sauce*
salt	25 g (1 oz) butter
2 onions, halved	7.5 ml (1½ tsp) plain flour
3–4 carrots, halved lengthways if large	1 egg yolk
2 celery sticks, halved lengthways	50 ml (2 fl oz) double cream
1 leek, halved lengthways	15–30 ml (1–2 tbsp) chopped large capers
2 bay leaves	finely chopped lemon rind, to garnish
6 black peppercorns, lightly crushed	
long strip of lemon rind	SERVES SIX

Put the meat into a large saucepan, add just enough water to cover and a sprinkling of salt. Bring to the boil, remove the scum from the surface and add the vegetables, bay leaves, peppercorns and lemon rind. Cover and simmer for 2½–3 hours until the meat is very tender. Transfer to a warmed plate and keep warm.

Melt half the butter, stir in the flour and cook for 1–2 minutes. Measure off 450 ml (16 fl oz) of the cooking liquor and gradually stir into the flour. Bring to the boil, stirring, then simmer until reduced to about 225 ml (8 fl oz) and slightly thickened.

Blend the egg yolk with the cream, blend in a little of the stock then pour back into the remaining stock and heat gently, stirring, until the sauce thickens – do not allow to boil. Stir in the capers and remaining butter. Adjust the seasoning, if necessary. Pour into a sauceboat and sprinkle the lemon rind over.

Serve the mutton, or lamb, carved into slices accompanied by the sauce.

Shepherd's Pie

Controversy surrounds this dish – should the meat be lamb or beef, should it be cooked or raw, when is the dish a shepherd's pie and when a cottage pie or are they the same? And the variety in the recipes is enormous – some are very simple and basic, others, like this one, have more flavour and character.

25 g (1 oz) butter	*Topping*
1 onion, finely chopped	400 g (14 oz) potatoes, cut into chunks
450 g (1 lb) lean beef, minced	225 g (8 oz) celeriac, cut into chunks
100 g (4 oz) mushrooms, chopped	40 g (1½ oz) butter, diced
15 ml (1 tbsp) tomato purée	2 eggs, separated
150 ml (¼ pint) red wine	SERVES FOUR TO SIX
150 ml (¼ pint) brown stock, preferably veal	
15 ml (1 tbsp) finely chopped fresh tarragon	
salt and pepper	

Melt the butter, add the onion and cook over a moderate heat until beginning to soften. Add the mince and cook, stirring frequently, until browned. Stir in the mushrooms, tomato purée, wine, stock, tarragon and seasoning. Cook gently for about 25 minutes, stirring occasionally.

Meanwhile, prepare the topping. Simmer the potatoes and celeriac until tender. Drain well and purée in a blender or food processor. Return to the rinsed out pan and heat gently, stirring, until dry. Beat in the butter, egg yolks and seasoning. Whisk the egg whites until stiff but not dry, then carefully fold into the purée.

Pour the meat into a deep 1.1 litre (2 pint) dish and cover with the potato. Bake at 200°C (400°F) mark 6 for about 30 minutes until the top is golden.

Parson's Venison

Marinating a leg of lamb in lightly spiced red wine transforms the flesh into a more full-flavoured meat reminiscent of venison.

25 g (1 oz) dripping or butter	*Marinade*
1 small onion, finely chopped	200 ml (7 fl oz) red wine
100 g (4 oz) mushrooms, chopped	75 ml (3 fl oz) tawny port
100 g (4 oz) ham, chopped	6 juniper berries, crushed
30 ml (2 tbsp) snipped chives	1.25 ml (¼ tsp) ground allspice
salt and pepper	30 ml (2 tbsp) vegetable oil
1.8–2 kg (4–4½ lb), leg of lamb, skinned and boned	45 ml (3 tbsp) red wine vinegar
	1 bay leaf
	1.25 ml (¼ tsp) freshly grated nutmeg

SERVES FOUR TO SIX

Melt half the dripping or butter, add the onion and mushrooms and cook, stirring frequently, until the onions are soft but not browned. Stir in the ham, chives and seasoning and leave to cool.

Season the lamb inside and out with black pepper, then spread the onion mixture over the inside. Roll up tightly and tie securely. Place in a casserole.

Mix the marinade ingredients together, pour over the lamb, cover and leave in a cool place for 24 hours, turning the joint over occasionally. Remove the meat from the marinade, drain and dry.

Melt the remaining dripping or butter in a flameproof casserole. Add the meat and brown on all sides over medium to high heat.

Pour in the marinade, bring meat almost to the boil, cover then cook at 180°C (350°F) mark 4 for 1¾–2 hours until the meat is tender, basting occasionally with the marinade.

Transfer the meat to a warmed plate. Skim the fat from the surface of the liquid, then boil the liquid rapidly until reduced and slightly thickened. Season and serve with the meat.

Oxtail Stew

This stew can be served as it is, straight from the pot with carrots, small onions and leeks.

25 g (1 oz) beef dripping,
  or vegetable oil
50 g (2 oz) bacon,
  chopped
1 large or 2 small oxtails,
  chopped
1 large onion, finely
  chopped
2 carrots, chopped
1 celery stick, chopped
1 large leek, chopped
bouquet garni of 1 bay
  leaf, sprig of thyme,
  4 parsley sprigs and a
  sprig of lovage
salt and pepper
300 ml (½ pint) brown ale
300 ml (½ pint) brown
  stock, preferably veal

finely chopped fresh
  parsley, to garnish

Dumplings
100 g (4 oz) self raising
  flour
salt and pepper
50 g (2 oz) shredded suet
  or cold diced butter
2.5 ml (½ tsp) creamed
  horseradish (optional)
30 ml (2 tbsp) water
225 ml (8 fl oz) brown
  stock, preferably veal,
  or water

SERVES FOUR

Heat the dripping or oil in a large flameproof casserole or heavy-based saucepan, add the bacon and oxtail pieces, a few at a time, and cook until beginning to brown. Remove with a slotted spoon and reserve.

Add the vegetables to the casserole or pan and cook over a low heat for about 3 minutes, stirring frequently, until the onion is beginning to soften but not brown.

Return the oxtail and bacon to the vegetables. Add the bouquet garni, seasoning, ale and stock and bring to the boil. Reduce the heat so the liquid barely moves, cover tightly and cook slowly for 2½–3 hours until the oxtail is very tender. Skim all fat off the surface.

About 25 minutes before the end of the cooking, combine all the ingredients for the dumplings except the stock and mix to a soft, but not sticky, dough with the water.

Divide into eight pieces and roll into small balls using floured hands. Bring the stock or water to the boil in a large saucepan; season if using water. Add the dumplings and poach for 15–20 minutes until cooked. Remove from the pan with a slotted spoon, draining well. Place the dumplings on top of the stew and sprinkle with parsley. Serve at once.

CROWN ROAST OF LAMB (page 53)

Traditional Roasts

THE roasts of England are famed through-out the world. Prior to the middle of the nineteenth century they were cooked over an open fire on a spit, with the spit being rotated by hand. In Tudor times, dogs were used, with clockwork mechanisms being intro-duced in the late eighteenth century. Roasting in the oven did not become common until the introduction of gas and electric stoves.

The best roast meat comes from a large joint so a roast is an obvious choice to serve when you have guests to feed. English roasts all have their traditional accompaniments – roast beef and Yorkshire pudding or horseradish sauce, lamb with mint sauce or redcurrant jelly, and pork with apple sauce.

Roast Beef and Yorkshire Pudding

Purists claim that Yorkshire pudding should be cooked beneath the meat, in the same tin so that it absorbs the maximum flavour, but, when made in this way, it will not be as light and crisp as when cooked separately. Using really hot fat helps to ensure light, crisp puddings. If preferred, a single large pudding can be made, but it will take about 35–40 minutes to cook.
Serve with mustard or horseradish sauce (see page 51) and roast potatoes (see page 71).

2.7 kg (6 lb) rib joint of beef with 3 ribs	pinch of salt
	1 egg, beaten
pepper	150 ml (¼ pint) milk
200 ml (7 fl oz) red wine	150 ml (¼ pint) water
Yorkshire puddings	SERVES SIX
100 g (4 oz) plain flour	

To make the Yorkshire pudding batter, sift the flour and salt into a bowl. Form a well in the centre, then pour in the egg and gradually draw in the flour. Add the milk and water and mix to a smooth batter. Leave to stand for 1–2 hours.

Sprinkle pepper over the beef, place on a rack in a roasting tin, then cook at 220°C(425°F) mark 7 for

20 minutes. Reduce the temperature to 190°C (375°F) mark 5 and cook for 20 minutes per 450 g (1 lb) for medium rare meat. Cook for 15 minutes less for rare meat; cook for 15 minutes longer for well done.

Ten minutes before the end of the cooking, pour off the surplus fat and put a little of it into 12 individual bun tins. Place in the hottest part of the oven for 5 minutes until really hot.

When the meat is done, leave it in a warm place, still on the rack and increase the oven temperature to 220°C (425°F) mark 7. Beat the batter and pour into the bun tins and cook for 15–20 minutes until risen, crisp and golden.

Place the roasting tin over a moderate heat and gradually stir the wine into the cooking juices, dislodging the sediment in the bottom of the tin. Bring to the boil and bubble for a few minutes. Season and pour into a warmed sauceboat.

Serve the beef with the Yorkshire puddings and with the gravy handed separately.

Roast Sirloin with Horseradish Sauce

This classic English dish is reputed to have been knighted by an English king after he had dined particularly well off a roasted loin of beef. For a meal 'fit for a king' serve with Yorkshire puddings (see page 50) and roast potatoes (see page 71).

1.1 kg (2½ lb) boned and rolled sirloin of beef
175 ml (6 fl oz) red wine
450 ml (¾ pint) brown stock, preferably veal
salt and pepper

Sauce
150 ml (¼ pint) whipping cream
45 ml (3 tbsp) freshly grated horseradish
about 22.5 ml (1½ tbsp) lemon juice

1.25–2.5 ml (¼–½ tsp) prepared English mustard
salt and white pepper
pinch of sugar (optional)

SERVES SIX

Place the meat, fat side up, on a rack placed in a roasting tin. Cook at 230°C (450°F) mark 8 for 15 minutes, then reduce the temperature to 170°C (325°F) mark 3 and cook for about a further 40 minutes for rare beef, basting once or twice.

Meanwhile, blend all the ingredients for the sauce and spoon into a serving bowl.

Leave the beef, still on the rack, in a warm place to settle. Drain off the excess fat from the roasting tin. Place the tin over a medium heat and stir in the red wine, dislodging the sediment stuck in the bottom of the tin.

Boil until almost completely evaporated, then stir in the stock and boil until reduced to 200 ml (7 fl oz). Season and pour into a sauceboat. Serve the beef accompanied by the gravy and horseradish sauce.

Roast Pork

To ensure crisp crackling, score right through the skin with a firm, sharp knife, following the grain of the meat, then rub the skin with vegetable or olive oil and coarse salt before cooking; never use previously frozen meat or the crackling will not work.

1.75 kg (3½ lb) loin of pork
vegetable oil and coarse salt
rosemary sprig
6 large Cox's Orange Pippin apples
salt and pepper
150 ml (¼ pint) dry white wine (optional)

150 ml (¼ pint) brown stock, preferably veal
watercress sprigs, to garnish

SERVES SIX TO EIGHT

Rub the skin of the pork with oil and then sprinkle with coarse salt. Place the rosemary on a rack in a roasting tin, put the pork on top and roast at 180°C (350°F) mark 4 for 2 hours.

Core the apples, season them inside and make a shallow cut through the skin around the apples about one third of the way down. Place in a tin or dish and baste with some of the fat from the pork. Cook on a lower shelf for the last 30 minutes of the cooking time.

Keep the pork warm on a rack. Drain off most of the fat from the roasting tin, leaving the meat juices. Stir in the wine, if using, dislodging the sediment. Boil until almost completely evaporated. Stir in stock and boil for 2–3 minutes. Strain into a sauceboat.

Arrange the apples around the pork, garnish with watercress and serve accompanied by the gravy.

Guard of Honour with Mint Sauce

If ordered in advance, the butcher will trim the racks of lamb. If the meat is from a very young lamb and the cutlets small it will probably be necessary to allow three per person.

---

2 best ends of lamb containing 6 cutlets each
100 ml (4 fl oz) red wine
150 ml (¼ pint) brown stock, preferably veal
salt and pepper
flageolet beans or broad beans and new potatoes, to serve
redcurrant jelly (see page 93), to serve

Sauce
60 ml (4 tbsp) finely chopped fresh mint
45 ml (3 tbsp) boiling water
30 ml (2 tbsp) caster sugar
60 ml (4 tbsp) white wine or wine vinegar
salt and pepper

SERVES SIX

Trim each cutlet bone to a depth of 5 cm (2 inches), then interlace the bones, fat side outwards, to form an arch. Tie the meat at intervals along the length and weave string between the bones to keep the joint in shape. Protect the tips of the bones with foil.

Place on a rack in a roasting tin and cook at 230°C (450°F) mark 8 for 10 minutes, then reduce the temperature to 180°C (350°F) mark 4 and cook for a further 25 minutes, basting occasionally.

To make the sauce, put the mint in a bowl, pour over the boiling water and leave for 20 minutes. Stir in the sugar, wine or wine vinegar and seasoning.

Remove the foil and leave the lamb, still on the rack, to rest for 15 minutes. Drain off the fat from the roasting tin. Stir in the wine and boil for a few minutes, then stir in the stock and boil for

2–3 minutes. Season, then pour into a sauceboat.

Transfer the lamb to a warmed serving plate and remove the trussing strings. Serve accompanied by the gravy, mint sauce, flageolet beans or broad beans, new potatoes and redcurrant jelly.

Crown Roast of Lamb

Order the joint 2 or 3 days in advance if you would like the butcher to prepare it for you. Ask him to include the trimmings with the joint. The stuffing may be cooked in the centre of the lamb but the cooking time will need to be longer, and the meat will not be rare. The apple and mint stuffing used here is soft and moist – for a firmer stuffing, double the quantity of breadcrumbs and add an egg.

2 best ends of lamb containing 6 cutlets each	450 g (1 lb) peeled and cored cooking apples (prepared weight)
15 g (½ oz) butter	50 g (2 oz) fresh breadcrumbs
1 small onion, halved	30 ml (2 tbsp) finely chopped mint
1 leek, halved	salt and pepper
1 carrot, halved	baby vegetables – peas,
1 celery stick, halved	small turnips, carrots,
5 black peppercorns	new potatoes, mange
200 ml (7 fl oz) dry white wine	tout, to serve
1.5 litres (2½ pints) water	
salt	

SERVES SIX

Stuffing
40 g (1½ oz) butter
2 shallots, finely chopped

Trim each cutlet bone to a depth of 5 cm (2 inches). Bend the joints around, fat side inwards, and sew together using strong cotton or fine string to form a crown.

Melt the butter in a saucepan, add the lamb trimmings and cook over a moderate heat until the fat melts and they colour very slightly.

Stir in the vegetables and cook for 2–3 minutes, stirring occasionally. Stir in the peppercorns, wine, water and salt. Bring to the boil, remove the scum from the surface, then simmer for 2–3 hours, removing the scum occasionally.

Strain the stock, leave to cool, then remove the fat from the surface. Boil the stock until reduced to about 300 ml (½ pint).

Place the crown roast on a rack in a roasting tin and cover the exposed bones with aluminium foil. Roast at 220°C (425°F) mark 7 for 15 minutes, then reduce the temperature to 180°C (350°F) mark 4. Tip any fat from the roasting tin and brush the joint with some of the stock. Return the roast to the oven and cook for 45–50 minutes, basting two or three times with the stock.

Meanwhile, prepare the stuffing. Heat 25 g (1 oz) of the butter, add the shallots, cover and cook for 3–4 minutes, shaking the pan occasionally until the shallots are softened but not coloured.

Stir in the apples and cook, stirring occasionally, until softened. Remove from the heat and stir in the breadcrumbs, mint and seasoning. Spoon into a buttered dish, dot the remaining butter on the top and cook in the oven for about 30 minutes.

Keep the lamb warm, still on the rack. Drain off the excess fat from the roasting tin leaving the juices behind. Stir in the remaining stock, dislodging the sediment. Bring to the boil and boil for 2–3 minutes.

Place the crown roast on a warmed serving plate, remove the foil, and spoon the stuffing into the centre. Pour the gravy into a small warmed jug and arrange baby vegetables around the meat.

Poultry and Game Dishes

A T ONE time almost every household in the town, village and country, kept at least a few chickens and these, along perhaps with some geese and ducks, would be the responsibility of the lady of the house, whether the house was a manor or a small cottage and whether she attended to the birds herself or directed someone else.

The birds provided eggs both for the household, and in country districts a little extra income. Generally the birds were not killed until they had ceased to lay economically, by which time they would be old, tough and frequently a little stringy. They would, however, have a good flavour and could be made into tasty dishes if cooked slowly. Young, tender birds were only killed if they were poor layers, or for a special occasion if the family could afford it.

The birds would roam around scratching for food, and different breeds became crossed with each other to produce new strains. By the 1850s some selective breeding experiments were begin-

ning to take place to produce breeds with specific characteristics, some for table use and some as layers. To keep them separate they were housed in cages and runs which, by the end of the nineteenth century, led to the first commercial poultry farms, and the beginnings of the poultry industry we have today.

← Game →

Game (birds and animals that are hunted and killed for sport as well as eating) was the province of the master of the house, from the king downwards. Since Saxon times the Crown had earmarked game preserves for itself and these lands were so extensive by the reign of Henry II, in the twelfth century, that they covered about one third of England. However, despite the severity of the punishments for poaching, which at times have been death or transportation, much game found its way on to the tables of those not included in the exclusive band of authorised consumers.

Partridges 'Stewed' with Red Wine and Anchovies

Anchovies used to be used quite frequently in meat, poultry and game dishes to enhance and enrich the dish without being allowed to dominate the other flavours. Cooked in this way older partridges – or other game birds, pigeon, hare or venison – become deliciously tender. The dish should traditionally be served with butter beans and Brussels sprouts for a warming winter dish.

1 onion, finely chopped
white part of 1 long thin
    leek, finely chopped
1 small carrot, finely
    chopped
bouquet garni of
    4 parsley sprigs, sprig
    of lovage, sprig of
    thyme and a small
    sprig of sage
2 partridges
450 ml (¾ pint) game
    stock

2 anchovy fillets
50 g (2 oz) unsalted butter
450 ml (¾ pint) claret or
    similar red wine
salt and pepper
croûtons dipped in
    chopped parsley, to
    garnish
butter beans and Brussels
    sprouts, to serve

SERVES FOUR TO SIX

Mix the vegetables together in a heavy flameproof casserole. Add the bouquet garni and partridges. Pour in the stock and bring to simmering point. Cover with aluminium foil and a lid and cook gently for about 1 hour.

Pound the anchovies with half the butter, then add to the casserole with the claret and seasoning. Bring to simmering point again, then re-cover with the foil and lid and cook for a further 1½ hours.

Transfer the partridges to a warmed serving plate and keep warm. Discard the bouquet garni and boil the liquid until reduced and slightly thickened. Pass through a sieve, if wished and reheat gently. Over a low heat, stir in the remaining butter and adjust the seasoning.

Pour the sauce over the partridges. Garnish with the croûtons and serve with butter beans and Brussels sprouts.

Salmi of Pheasant

*This is a classic example of a very good,
traditional English dish, a salomene, having its
name changed to a French one for reasons of
culinary snobbery. Although it can be made
with left-over pheasant, or other game, it is best
to use birds that have been specifically cooked
for this recipe. Preparation is quicker if 450 ml
(¾ pint) ready-prepared game stock is used.*

2 young pheasants, oven-
   ready
salt and pepper
2 thyme sprigs
2 bacon slices
1 onion, halved
1 large carrot, quartered
450 ml (¾ pint) red wine
1.1 litre (2 pints) brown
   stock, preferably veal

bouquet garni of sprig of
   parsley, sprig of thyme,
   small sprig of rosemary
   and a bay leaf
65 g (2½ oz) butter
2 shallots, finely chopped
15 ml (1 tbsp) plain flour
100 g (4 oz) mushrooms
croûtons and chopped
   fresh parsley, to
   garnish

SERVES FOUR

Season the pheasants, place a sprig of thyme in the
cavity of each and tie a slice of bacon over the
breasts. Place in a roasting tin just large enough to
hold them and roast for 25 minutes at 230°C (450°F)
mark 8. Leave the oven on.

Remove the bacon and trussing strings. Remove
and reserve the skin and divide the birds into joints.
Carefully remove the flesh from the bones and
carcass. Place the flesh in a casserole.

Chop the bones and skin and put into a roasting
tin with the onion and carrot. Cook in the oven for
about 10 minutes, stirring occasionally, until

browned. Tip the bones, skin and vegetables into a
large saucepan. Stir 300 ml (½ pint) of the wine into
the roasting tin to dislodge the sediment, bring to
the boil then pour into the saucepan.

Add the veal stock, bring to the boil, remove the
scum from the surface, add the bouquet garni and
simmer for about 2 hours, removing the scum from
the surface occasionally.

Strain through a sieve, pressing down well on the
bones and vegetables to extract as much liquid as
possible. Measure the liquid – there should be about
450 ml (¾ pint).

Melt 40 g (1½ oz) of the butter in a saucepan, add
the shallots, cover and cook, shaking the pan
occasionally, until softened but not browned. Stir in
the flour then gradually stir in the stock. Bring to the
boil, stirring, then simmer for about 20 minutes.

Meanwhile, boil the remaining wine until reduced
to 15 ml (1 tbsp). Cook the mushrooms in the
remaining butter.

Stir the sauce into the reduced wine and bring to
the boil. Adjust the seasoning. Pour over the
pheasant, moving the pieces carefully to make sure
they are all covered with the sauce. Stir in the
mushrooms. Cover and heat through at 180°C
(350°F) mark 4 for about 15–20 minutes.

Transfer to a warmed serving plate and garnish
with the croûtons and parsley.

SALMI OF PHEASANT (above)

Cornish Caudle Chicken Pie

Caudle refers to the cream and egg mixture that is poured into the pie near the end of the cooking. The quantity of pastry will give just a thin covering, a larger amount can be used if preferred.

50 g (2 oz) butter
1 onion, finely chopped
4 chicken legs, about
   100 g (4 oz) each, boned
20 g (¾ oz) fresh parsley
   leaves, finely chopped
4 spring onions, chopped
salt and pepper
150 ml (¼ pt) milk

150 ml (¼ pt) soured
   cream
puff pastry made with
   100 g (4 oz) plain flour
beaten egg, for glazing
150 ml (¼ pt) double
   cream
1 egg, beaten

SERVES FOUR

Melt half the butter in a frying pan, add the onion and cook over a low heat, stirring occasionally, until softened but not browned. Transfer to a 1.1 litre (2 pint) pie dish using a slotted spoon.

Add the remaining butter to the pan, add the chicken and cook until evenly browned. Arrange on top of the onion in a single layer. Stir the parsley, spring onions, seasoning, milk and soured cream into the pan and bring to the boil. Simmer for 2–3 minutes, then pour over the chicken.

Cover with foil and cook at 180°C (350°F) mark 4 for about 30 minutes. Remove from the oven and leave to cool.

Meanwhile, roll out the pastry on a lightly floured surface until about 2.5 cm (1 inch) larger all round than the pie dish. Leave the pastry to relax whilst the filling is cooling.

Cut off a strip from all round the edge of the pastry. Place the strip on the rim of the pie dish, moisten, then place the pastry lid on top. Crimp the edges, make a small hole in the top and insert a small funnel of aluminium foil.

Brush the top of the pie with beaten egg and bake for 15–20 minutes at 220°C (425°F) mark 7 until a light golden brown. Reduce the temperature to 180°C (350°F) mark 4.

Beat the cream into the egg, then strain into a jug and pour into the pie through the foil funnel. Remove the funnel, shake the dish to distribute the cream and return the pie to the oven for about 5 minutes. Remove from the oven and leave to stand in a warm place for 5–10 minutes before serving warm, or leave to cool completely and serve cold.

Pigeons in a Pot with Plums

Pigeon are particularly plentiful in the countryside in the autumn, especially in corn growing regions, just at the time when plums are ripe. This dish from Kent happily combines the two.

15 g (½ oz) butter
4 young pigeons,
   prepared
10 ml (2 tsp) plain flour
   seasoned with a pinch
   of grated nutmeg
1 onion, chopped
2 cloves
5 ml (1 tsp) finely
   chopped fresh
   rosemary

5 ml (1 tsp) finely
   chopped fresh thyme
2.5 ml (½ tsp) finely
   chopped fresh sage
100 ml (4 fl oz) port
450 g (1 lb) purple plums,
   stoned and halved

SERVES FOUR

Melt the butter in a frying pan. Coat the pigeons lightly in the flour, then add to the pan and fry, turning occasionally, until lightly browned. Transfer to an ovenproof casserole.

Stir the onion into the frying pan and fry gently until beginning to soften. Spoon over the pigeons and sprinkle the cloves and herbs over the top.

Stir the port into the frying pan, bring to the boil, then pour over the pigeons. Arrange the plums over the top. Cover tightly and cook at 170°C (325°F) mark 3 for 1½ hours until the pigeons are tender.

Transfer the pigeons and plums to a warmed large serving platter. Boil the juices to thicken them and concentrate the flavour. Pour over the pigeons.

Roast Haunch of Venison

Venison is a very lean meat. Marinating, then wrapping in a simple flour or 'huff' paste, help to keep it moist and succulent.

1 small haunch of
  venison, about 1.8 kg
  (4 lb)
50 ml (2 fl oz) vegetable
  oil
3 shallots, chopped
1 carrot, chopped
1 bay leaf
sprig of marjoram
2 parsley sprigs
10 black peppercorns,
  lightly crushed
8 juniper berries

600 ml (1 pint) red wine
500 g (1¼ lb) plain flour
about 300 ml (½ pint)
  water
50 g (2 oz) butter,
  softened
redcurrant jelly (see
  page 93) or
  Cumberland sauce (see
  page 94), to serve

SERVES SIX

Put the venison into a large dish. Mix the oil, shallots, carrot, bay leaf, marjoram, parsley, peppercorns, juniper berries and wine together and pour over the venison. Cover and leave in a cool place for 24 hours, basting the meat occasionally and turning it over two or three times. Remove the venison from the marinade, drain and dry it well. Reserve the marinade.

Mix the flour to a stiff paste with the water. Roll out to about 1 cm (½ inch) thick. Spread the butter over the venison, then encase the joint in the paste, dampening the edges and pressing them together well to seal them.

Wrap in brown paper or a double thickness of greaseproof paper. Place in a roasting tin and cook at 230°C (450°F) mark 8 for 15 minutes. Reduce the temperature to 170°C (325°F) mark 3 and cook for 20 minutes per 450 g (1 lb).

About 30 minutes before the end of the cooking time, remove and discard the paper and the crust. Raise the oven temperature to 220°C (425°F) mark 7, baste the venison with some of the marinade, and complete the cooking, basting twice more.

Transfer to a rack on a warmed plate and keep warm. Place the roasting tin over a moderately high heat, gradually add 225 ml (8 fl oz) of the marinade, stirring to dislodge the sediment. Bring to the boil and boil for a few minutes. Pour into a warmed sauceboat and serve with the venison accompanied by redcurrant jelly or Cumberland sauce.

Douce Ame

This recipe is based upon one that appeared in the 'Forme of Cury' (Manner of Cookery), one of the earliest collections of manuscript recipes, written about 1390 by Richard II's cooks.

1.5 kg (3 lb) chicken, jointed	2.5 ml (½ tsp) chopped hyssop (or use an extra
seasoned flour	½ sage leaf and a small
25 g (1 oz) butter	pinch of chopped fresh
600 ml (1 pt) milk	mint)
about 40 g (1½ oz) clear honey	2.5 ml (½ tsp) finely chopped summer
45 ml (3 tbsp) chopped fresh parsley	savory
2 small sage leaves, finely chopped	pinch of ground saffron salt and pepper
	50 g (2 oz) pine nuts

SERVES FOUR TO SIX

Lightly coat the pieces of chicken in seasoned flour. Melt the butter in a heavy flameproof casserole, add the chicken and cook over a medium heat until golden brown.

Blend the milk, honey, herbs, saffron and seasoning together. Lift the chicken out of the casserole and stir the flavoured milk into the juices, dislodging the sediment. Bring to the boil, then add the chicken, turning the pieces to coat them in the liquid. Cover and cook over a low heat for about 40 minutes – the water should barely move.

Lift the pieces of chicken from the liquid and remove the skin. Boil the liquid to reduce it slightly and concentrate the flavour. Adjust the seasoning. Add pine nuts and return chicken to the casserole.

Duckling with Green Peas

This particular recipe for the well-known combination of duckling and green peas is much less fatty than some, yet the vegetables still have plenty of flavour. Use a fresh, free-range duckling for the best results. If fresh peas are not available, frozen ones can be substituted. There is no need to blanch them.

2–2.3 kg (4½–5 lb) duckling	50 g (2 oz) smoked streaky bacon, diced
40 g (1½ oz) butter	60 ml (4 tbsp) veal stock
12–15 pickling or small onions	2 summer savory sprigs salt and pepper
450g (1 lb) shelled peas	

SERVES FOUR TO FIVE

Prick the skin of the duck, taking care not to pierce the flesh. Place on a rack in a roasting tin and cook at 220°C (425°F) mark 7 for 40 minutes.

Melt the butter in a saucepan, add the onions and cook turning frequently until lightly browned. Blanch peas for 3 minutes, refresh and drain well. Blanch the bacon for 1 minute, rinse and drain well.

Pour the surplus fat from the roasting tin then stir the stock into the sediment. Mix the peas, bacon, onions and savory together, place around the duck, season the duck and vegetables and cook at 170°C (325°F) mark 3 for about 20–30 minutes until the duck is cooked and the juices run clear when the thickest part of the leg is pierced with a fine skewer.

Serve the duck surrounded by the vegetables and with the cooking juices.

DUCKLING WITH GREEN PEAS (above)

Michaelmas Goose

Queen Elizabeth I ordered that roast goose should be served in commemoration of the defeat of the Spanish Armada on Michaelmas Day. A Michaelmas goose, fattened on the gleanings from the cornfields, was less fatty than a Christmas bird. It was customarily served with other foods available at the same time – the first wind-fall apples and Fermenty pudding made from the new corn.

3.5–4.5 kg (8–10 lb) goose, trussed weight	finely grated rind and juice of 1 lemon
salt and pepper	
	Sauce
Stuffing	450 g (lb) cooking apples
50 g (2 oz) butter	25 g (1 oz) unsalted butter
2 onions, finely chopped	25–50 g (1–2 oz) sugar
the goose liver, finely chopped	2 cloves or a pinch of freshly grated nutmeg
45 ml (3 tbsp) finely chopped fresh sage	15 ml (1 tbsp) water
175 g (6 oz) fresh white breadcrumbs	SERVES SIX TO EIGHT

To make the stuffing, melt the butter, add the onions and cook gently, stirring occasionally, until softened but not browned. Stir in the liver and cook until it just begins to stiffen and change colour. Remove from the heat and stir in the sage, breadcrumbs, lemon rind and juice and seasoning.

Remove any lumps of fat from the cavity of the goose, then season it well inside and out. Spoon the stuffing into the neck end. Do not pack the stuffing too tightly. If there is too much stuffing, put the extra in a roasting tin and cook in the oven

30 minutes before the end of the cooking time.

Truss the goose neatly, then prick the breasts, sides and legs. Place the bird, breast side up, on a rack in a roasting tin and cook at 220°C (425°F) mark 7 for 20 minutes.

Turn the goose over. Reduce the temperature to 170°C (325°F) mark 3 and cook for 1 hour. Turn the goose over again on to its back and cook for about 1 hour until the juices run clear when the thickest part of the leg is pierced with a skewer. Pour off the fat several times during the cooking.

Meanwhile, make the apple sauce. Put the apples, butter, sugar, cloves or nutmeg and water in a saucepan, cover and cook gently until soft. Beat to a smooth purée.

Leave the goose to stand in a warm place for 15 minutes before carving. Serve with the apple sauce.

Rabbit in the Dairy

This is a sympathetic method of cooking young rabbit that works equally well with chicken joints. It is pale, but is deliberately left ungarnished so as not to detract from the delicate flavour. Instead, serve it on a colourful plate. Young broad beans and new potatoes cooked in their skins are good accompaniments.

1 small celery stick, finely chopped	salt and white pepper
1 shallot, finely chopped	2 fresh bay leaves
25 g (1 oz) cooked ham, finely chopped	300 ml (½ pint) milk
1 young rabbit, jointed	SERVES FOUR

Arrange the celery, shallot and ham in a heavy earthenware casserole. Place the pieces of rabbit on top, season and add the bay leaves.

Bring the milk to the boil and pour over the rabbit. Cover tightly and cook at 170°C (325°F) mark 3 for about 2 hours until the rabbit is tender.

Strain off the cooking liquid and boil to reduce slightly. Taste and adjust the seasoning. Transfer the rabbit, vegetables and ham to a warmed serving plate or dish and pour the liquid over.

Edgurdouce

Conyng (coney or mature rabbit) was very popular in medieval times and is featured in many recipes from that time. It was rated so highly as a meat that it was served at the coronation feast of Henry IV in 1399. This recipe is typical of the sweet spiciness of dishes then. Use dried apricots without added sulphur dioxide.

300 ml (½ pint) sweet wine
45 ml (3 tbsp) red wine vinegar
175 g (6 oz) seedless muscatel raisins
175 g (6 oz) dried apricots
5 ml (1 tsp) ground ginger
5 ml (1 tsp) ground cinnamon
a small piece of fresh root ginger, very finely chopped

4 cloves
4 juniper berries, lightly crushed
salt and white pepper
4 rabbit joints
flour, for coating
22.5 ml (1½ tbsp) olive oil
orange segments, pith and peel removed, and finely shredded stem ginger, to garnish

SERVES FOUR

Gently warm the wine and vinegar to simmering point, then pour over the raisins and apricots in a bowl. Add the spices and seasoning, stir, cover and leave overnight.

Add the rabbit portions to the fruits and liquid, turn them over to coat in the liquid, then cover and leave in a cool place for about 6 hours, turning occasionally.

Dry the rabbit portions with absorbent kitchen paper and coat lightly in flour. Heat the oil in a heavy flameproof casserole, add the rabbit and fry until a light golden brown. Drain on absorbent kitchen paper.

Pour off any excess oil from the casserole, then stir in the wine and fruit and bring to the boil. Return the rabbit to the casserole, cover with foil and a lid and cook for about 40 minutes until the rabbit is tender – the liquid should hardly move.

Transfer the rabbit to a warmed serving plate and keep warm. Boil the liquid until reduced and thickened, then pour over the rabbit.

Serve garnished with orange segments and finely shredded ginger.

Game Pie

*A delicious cold pie that is traditionally packed
as part of the lunch for shooting parties. It is
also ideal for any winter packed meal, buffet or
a special cold meal.*

1 pheasant
1 grouse
1 partridge
1 pigeon
225 g (8 oz) belly of pork,
 rinded
100 g (4 oz) salt pork or
 streaky bacon, rinded
2 shallots
hot water crust pastry
 made with 450 g (1 lb)
 flour
salt and pepper
beaten egg, to glaze
10 ml (2 tsp) powdered
 gelatine
Cumberland sauce, to
 serve (page 94)

Marinade
300 ml (½ pint) red wine
25 ml (1 fl oz) brandy

50 ml (2 fl oz) oil
8 juniper berries, crushed
3 parsley sprigs
3 thyme sprigs
1 bay leaf
2 sage leaves
blade of mace

Stock
1 onion, chopped
1 carrot, chopped
1 celery stick, chopped
150 ml (¼ pint) white
 wine
450 ml (¾ pint) chicken
 stock
6 juniper berries
bouquet garni of 1 bay
 leaf, 4 parsley sprigs,
 sprig of thyme and
 small sprig of rosemary

SERVES EIGHT

Remove and reserve the skin from the birds.
Remove and discard the fat. Carefully remove the
breasts from each bird with a sharp knife, cutting
away as much of the remaining flesh as possible
from the bones. Cut the flesh into approximately
2 cm (¾ inch) pieces. Chop the carcasses and bones.
 Mince the belly of pork, salt pork or bacon and

shallots together and mix with the game flesh. Put in
a large earthenware dish. Mix the marinade
ingredients together, pour into the dish, stir lightly
to mix, cover and leave in a cool place for 24 hours,
turning the flesh over occasionally.
 Meanwhile, put the carcasses, skin and bones into
a roasting tin and brown in the oven at 220°C (425°F)
mark 7 for 20 minutes. Add the onion, carrot and
celery for the stock, turning them over to coat in the
juices in the tin, and cook for 10 minutes.
 Transfer the carcasses, bones and vegetables to a
large saucepan. Place the roasting tin over a medium
heat, add the wine and stir to dislodge the sediment.
Bring to the boil, then pour into the saucepan. Add
the stock, juniper berries and bouquet garni and
bring to the boil.
 Remove the scum from the surface, then simmer
for 2 hours, removing the scum occasionally. Pass
through a conical strainer. Reduce to 450 ml (¾ pint).
 Leave to cool, then remove the fat from the
surface. Drain the liquid from the meats and dry the
meats well on absorbent kitchen paper.
 Roll out two-thirds of the pastry and use to line
the base and sides of a 23 cm (9 inch) raised pie
mould or drop-sided tin, leaving a slight overlap all
the way round. Spoon the meats into the pastry
case, seasoning them well.
 Roll out the remaining pastry to form a lid and
cover the pie. Press the edges well to seal them,
then trim off the excess pastry. Scallop the edges.
Make a small hole in the centre of the lid and insert
a small funnel of aluminium foil. Decorate the pie,
then brush the top with beaten egg.
 Bake at 200°C (400°F) mark 6 for 20 minutes, then
reduce the temperature to 180°C (350°F) mark 4 and
cook for a further 1½ hours. Remove the sides of the
tin, or unfasten them. Brush the pie all over with
beaten egg and return to the oven for
15–20 minutes. To check if the filling is cooked,
insert a skewer into the centre of the pie. Leave for ☞

CORNISH CAUDLE CHICKEN PIE (page 58)

10 seconds, then remove the skewer; it should be hot. If not, brush the pie with more beaten egg and return it to the oven for a further 15 minutes.

Leave the pie on a wire rack until almost cold.

Sprinkle the gelatine over a little of the stock and leave for 2 minutes. Stir in the remaining stock and heat gently, stirring, until the gelatine has dissolved. Cool until it is just becoming a light syrupy consistency, then pour through a funnel placed in the lid of the pie.

Leave the pie in a cool place overnight. Return to room temperature 2 hours before serving.

Jugged Hare

This dish gets its name from the earthenware jug-type cooking pot that was used for cooking older, tougher hare for a long time on the hearth beside a large open fire. Order the hare a few days in advance; ask for the blood.

150 g (5 oz) streaky bacon, diced	salt and pepper
50 g (2 oz) butter	150 ml (¼ pint) red wine
1 large hare, jointed, with its blood	75 ml (3 fl oz) ruby port
12 small onions	200 ml (7 fl oz) game stock
2 celery sticks, sliced	lemon juice (optional)
2 carrots, chopped	croûtons and parsley sprigs, to garnish
bouquet garni of 1 bay leaf, small sprig of rosemary, 6 parsley stalks, sprig of thyme and 2 sage leaves	redcurrant jelly (see page 93) and boiled potatoes, to serve
blade of mace, 6 peppercorns and 6 cloves, tied in muslin	SERVES SIX TO EIGHT

Heat the bacon gently in a heavy flameproof casserole until the fat runs, then add the butter. When it has melted, add the hare joints and cook until an even light mahogany brown. Remove with a slotted spoon and keep warm.

Add the vegetables to the casserole and fry, stirring occasionally, until the onions are lightly browned.

Pour off any excess fat and return the hare to the casserole. Add the bouquet garni, muslin bag and seasoning. Cover tightly with foil then a lid.

Stand the casserole in a larger one containing sufficient boiling water to come just above the height of the ingredients in the first pot. Cover tightly and simmer gently, replenishing the water as necessary, for about 3 hours until the hare is tender.

Transfer the hare and vegetables to a warmed serving plate and keep warm. Strain the juices, add the wine and port and boil until reduced to 50 ml (2 fl oz). Add the stock and simmer for 5 minutes. Reduce the heat.

Allow a little of the liquid to cool, then stir it into the blood. Pour back into the pan. Heat gently, stirring until thickened but do not allow it to boil. Season and add lemon juice, if necessary.

Spoon over the sauce and garnish. Serve with redcurrant jelly and potatoes.

Vegetables

IN A society that considers the consumption of flesh an indication of wealth and prestige, vegetables have always played a secondary role to game, meat and poultry.

However vegetables did formerly play a larger part in the diet of country folk and the poor than they do today, and even in the homes of the ordinary middle classes vegetables would be made into tasty family dishes such as ragoos. Any roots, leafy vegetables or shoots that grew wild, or could be cultivated easily on a plot of land, were a valued source of food.

Onions, leeks, garlic and cabbage were the most common early vegetables, with herbs being used far more widely, and in much greater variety than is common practice today – some early salads were composed almost exclusively of different types of fresh herbs.

With the increase of travelling more and more varieties of vegetables were introduced from abroad. Some that we consider quite unusual or new today were in popular use years ago, such as globe and Jerusalem artichokes, asparagus and salsify. Celery and cucumber were cooked for serving as vegetables.

Commercial market gardening began in the seventeenth century around London and the south east, but did not really begin to develop on any scale until the eighteenth and nineteenth centuries. It remained restricted to the southern counties until improved transportation enabled produce to be carried further north.

An Eighteenth Century Fine Salad

In the days when salads often contained meat, fish or chicken, this would have been considered a very simple salad. But even so, it would have been arranged attractively.

---

1 crisp lettuce
2 large or 4 small cooked
    artichoke bottoms,
    diced
750 g (1½ lb) thin
    asparagus spears,
    cooked and trimmed to
    10 cm (4 inches)
crisp croûtons fried in
    butter, to serve
finely chopped fresh
    chervil and chervil
    sprigs, to garnish

Dressing
1 small egg yolk
2 small lightly hard-
    boiled egg yolks,
    sieved
salt and white pepper
pinch of cayenne pepper
pinch of sugar
about 10 ml (2 tsp) lemon
    juice or herb vinegar
150 ml (¼ pint) double
    cream

SERVES FOUR TO SIX

First prepare the dressing. Stir the raw egg yolk into the hard-boiled egg yolks, then stir in the seasonings, sugar and lemon juice or vinegar. Gradually stir in the cream. Taste and add more lemon juice or vinegar and seasonings, if necessary.

Wash and dry the lettuce leaves and arrange on a large platter with the artichoke bottoms, and asparagus spears. Place the dressing in the centre.

Scatter warm croûtons over and garnish with finely chopped chervil and sprigs of chervil.

AN EIGHTEENTH CENTURY FINE SALAD (above)

Bubble and Squeak

The story behind the name of this dish is that the boiled beef and boiled vegetables originally used, bubbled in the water and squeaked when they were fried.

40 g (1½ oz) dripping or
  bacon fat
4 or 8 slices of boiled or
  otherwise cooked beef
1 onion, finely chopped
450 g (1 lb) potatoes,
  cooked and mashed

225 g (8 oz) cooked
  cabbage, finely
  chopped
salt and pepper

SERVES FOUR

Heat the dripping or bacon fat in a frying pan. Add the slices of beef and cook until lightly browned on both sides. Drain on absorbent kitchen paper and keep warm.

Add the onion to the pan and cook, stirring frequently, until softened. Remove with a slotted spoon and mix with the potatoes, cabbage and seasoning. Spoon this mixture into the frying pan and flatten it out to make a large flat cake.

Fry over medium heat for about 15 minutes until browned underneath. Turn the cake over and brown the other side. Cut into wedges or pieces and serve beside the beef.

Pease Pudding

Pease pudding, from the north of England, is served with pork or bacon. Instead of the final baking used here, the purée can be returned to the cloth and boiled for a further 45 minutes. Cold pease pudding can be sliced and fried in bacon fat.

225 g (8 oz) yellow split
  peas, soaked overnight
  and drained
50 g (2 oz) bacon,
  chopped
1 onion, quartered
1 carrot, halved
bouquet garni of 1 bay
  leaf, 4 parsley stalks,
  sprig of thyme and
  2 sage leaves

50 g (2 oz) butter
1 egg, beaten
pinch of sugar
salt and pepper

SERVES FOUR TO SIX

Tie the peas in a cloth leaving plenty of room for them to swell. Put into a large saucepan with the bacon, onion, carrot and bouquet garni. Cover with water, bring to the boil and boil for 10 minutes, then lower the heat, cover and simmer the pudding for about 2½ hours.

Tip the peas out of the cloth and press through a sieve, using a wooden spoon.

Beat in half the butter, the egg, a pinch of sugar and the seasoning. Spoon into a buttered dish, dot with the remaining butter and bake for 30 minutes at 200°C (400°F) mark 6.

Pan Haggerty

*A tasty potato dish from Northumberland
which can be served for supper or high tea.*

50 g (2 oz) beef dripping or bacon fat	100 g (4 oz) Cheddar cheese, grated
450 g (1 lb) firm potatoes, sliced very thinly	salt and pepper
225 g (8 oz) onions, thinly sliced	SERVES FOUR

Melt the dripping or bacon fat in a large, heavy
frying pan. Remove the pan from the heat and
arrange the potatoes, onions and cheese in alternate
layers, starting and ending with potatoes, and
seasoning the layers with salt and pepper.

Cook for about 30 minutes over low heat at first,
then over higher heat so that the underneath of the
mixture browns.

Place under a hot grill for 5–10 minutes to brown
the top layer of potatoes.

Roast Potatoes

*For crisp roast potatoes, they must be
thoroughly dry and put into very hot fat.*

550 g (1¼ lb) potatoes, cut into halves or large chunks	fat from the joint, or dripping
	SERVES FOUR

Cook the potatoes in lightly salted simmering water
for about 7 minutes. Drain well and dry on
absorbent kitchen paper.

Pour some of the fat from around the joint into a
separate tin, or put the dripping into the tin and
return to the oven so that it becomes really hot.

Put the potatoes into the fat, turn them over so
they are coated in fat and roast at 200°–220°C
(400°–425°F) mark 6–7 for about 40 minutes until
crisp and golden.

Puddings

TO THE English, pudding generally refers to hot, sweet dishes such as crumbles, rice and other cereal puddings, baked and steamed sponge, suet mixtures, pies, tarts and other pastries, pancakes and fritters. It may also include all cold sweet dishes that are served at the end of a meal – trifle, fruit fools, syllabubs, jellies and even ice creams, but these are normally called desserts rather than puddings.

The very first puddings and pies were, in fact, savoury dishes, although many contained sweet ingredients, spices and fruits. But by the middle of the seventeenth century they began to become more sweet as sugar became cheaper and more readily available.

By the beginning of the eighteenth century, pudding usually meant a dish that was based on sugar, flour and suet, often with fruits, spices and eggs added. Under the patronage of George I, nicknamed the pudding king, recipes for very sweet, rich and often heavy, puddings increased enormously, with nearly every town or village, profession or occupation, notable occasion and even battle having a pudding named after it.

Until the beginning of the nineteenth century puddings and pies were served as part of the second and third courses alongside savoury dishes, but with the gradual defining of courses, they began to take their place at the end of the meal, joining the elaborate moulded sweets and jellies, the fanciful confections and cakes, the carved creations of iced desserts, preserves and fruits, that had their hey-day with the French influence during Victoria's reign.

BOODLES ORANGE FOOL (page 74)

Port Jelly

Prior to the introduction of flavoured jelly tablets, jellies were serious desserts, and in the fifteenth and sixteenth centuries they were often set in elaborate moulds and served, shimmering, on silver salvers.

rind of 1 lemon and 1 orange in long strips	1 cinnamon stick
juice of 1 lemon	1 egg white, lightly beaten
100 g (4 oz) sugar	2 egg shells, crushed
250 ml (9 fl oz) water	300 ml (½ pint) ruby port
15 ml (1 tbsp) powdered gelatine	
15 ml (1 tbsp) redcurrant jelly (see page 93)	SERVES FOUR

Scald all the equipment to be used for the jelly.

Place the lemon and orange rind, lemon juice, sugar and 200 ml (7 fl oz) water in a saucepan and heat gently, stirring, until the sugar has dissolved.

Sprinkle the gelatine over 50 ml (2 fl oz) water in a bowl and leave to soften for 2 minutes. Stand in a saucepan of hot water and stir until the gelatine has dissolved.

Stir into the sugar syrup with the redcurrant jelly and cinnamon. Whisk in the egg white and shells and continue whisking until the mixture comes to the boil.

Stop whisking as the foam begins to rise and remove the pan from the heat. Return the pan to the heat and repeat this procedure twice, allowing the foam to rise and fall without any further whisking. Cool for 10 minutes.

Pour the jelly through a jelly bag or sieve lined with a double thickness of muslin or cheesecloth, into a basin – do not press it through or it will cloud the jelly, but allow it to drip naturally.

Stir in the port, then pour into a dampened 600 ml (1 pint) jelly mould and leave to set in a cool place for at least 4 hours.

To serve, dip the mould up to the rim in hot water for 5 seconds, then place a plate upside down over the mould. Invert the two, giving them a good shake, then lift off the mould.

Boodles Orange Fool

A speciality of Boodles Club, a gentleman's club in London's St. James'.

100 g (4 oz) sponge cake, broken into pieces	150 ml (¼ pint) double cream
finely grated rind of 2 oranges and 1 lemon	whipped cream and orange slices, to decorate
juice of 4 oranges and 2 lemons	
40–50 g (1½–2 oz) caster sugar	SERVES FOUR TO SIX

Arrange the pieces of sponge cake in the base of a glass serving dish. Stir the fruit rinds and juices with the sugar until the sugar has dissolved.

Whip the cream until thick but not stiff, then slowly whip in the fruit juice and rinds. Spoon over the sponge cakes and leave in a cool place until the juices have seeped into and soaked the sponge cakes.

Decorate with whipped cream and orange slices.

Eton Mess

The annual prize giving at Eton College – one of England's foremost public schools – is held on the 4th June. On that day, parents and pupils picnic on the famous playing fields with this luscious dish as part of their meal.

450 g (1 lb) strawberries
75 ml (3 fl oz) Kirsch
450 ml (¾ pint) double or
   whipping cream

6 meringues, crushed

SERVES FOUR TO SIX

Reserve a few small strawberries, chop the remainder and place in a bowl. Sprinkle the Kirsch over, cover and chill for 2–3 hours.

Whip the cream until it stands in soft peaks. Gently fold in the strawberries and their juices and the meringues.

Spoon into a glass serving dish, decorate with the reserved strawberries and serve immediately.

Summer Pudding

Summer Pudding was created in the eighteenth century as an alternative to the rich pastry desserts that were then fashionable. Any combination of mixed summer red berries and currants can be used.

900 g (2 lb) blackcurrants,
   redcurrants,
   raspberries,
   loganberries,
   strawberries,
   blackberries
about 150 g (5 oz) caster
   sugar

about 8 thin slices of
   bread, crusts removed
cream, or plain yogurt, to
   serve

SERVES SIX

Put the fruit in a bowl, sprinkle the sugar over, cover and leave overnight. Put the fruit and juice into a saucepan, then heat gently for 2–3 minutes. Taste and add more sugar if necessary.

Cut some of the bread into wedge shapes to fit into the bottom of a 1.1 litre (2 pint) pudding basin. Cut and arrange the remaining bread so that it lines the bowl neatly with no spaces between the slices.

Fill with the fruit and most of the juice, then cover the fruit completely with a layer of bread. Spoon the remaining juice over the top layer of bread. Place a plate that just fits inside the basin on top of the pudding. Put one or more weights on top and leave in a cool place overnight.

To serve, carefully run a knife between the pudding and the bowl, then invert on to a serving plate. Serve with cream or plain yogurt.

Trifle

In eighteenth century recipes a syllabub mixture was used to cover the custard, rather than the cream, and fruit was not included.

50 g (2 oz) ratafias, lightly crushed	*Topping*
50 g (2 oz) macaroons, lightly crushed	75 ml (3 fl oz) dessert wine
65 ml (2½ fl oz) dessert wine	15 ml (1 tbsp) cognac
15 ml (1 tbsp) orange liqueur	freshly grated rind and juice of ½ a lemon
300 ml (½ pint) single cream	25 g (1 oz) caster sugar
vanilla pod	175 ml (6 fl oz) double cream
4 egg yolks	crystallised violets and roses, to decorate
25 g (1 oz) caster sugar	SERVES FOUR TO SIX

Mix together the first three ingredients for the topping in a bowl and leave overnight.

Mix the ratafias and macaroons in a glass bowl and sprinkle with the wine and liqueur. Leave to soak. Gently heat the single cream with the vanilla pod to simmering point. Remove from the heat, cover and leave to infuse for about 20 minutes. Remove the vanilla pod.

Blend the egg yolks with the sugar. Stir in a little of the cream, then pour back into the bulk of the cream. Cook over a low heat, stirring constantly, until the sauce thickens – do not allow it to boil. Leave to cool, stirring occasionally to prevent a skin forming, then strain over the ratafias and macaroons and leave to set.

Strain the liquid for the topping and stir in the sugar, stirring until it has dissolved. Slowly stir in the double cream, then whisk lightly with a balloon whisk until the topping just holds its shape. Spread over the set custard.

Cover and leave in a cool place overnight. Decorate with crystallised violets and roses just before serving.

Fruit Crumble

Fruit crumbles are high on the list of favourite English puddings. They are extremely simple to make and any type of fruit that grows wild or in the garden can be used.

700 g (1½ lb) raw fruit, eg blackberries, apples, plums, rhubarb, prepared and sliced according to type	50 g (2 oz) hard butter or margarine, chopped
100–175 g (4–6 oz) caster sugar	50 g (2 oz) Demerara sugar
100 g (4 oz) plain flour	custard (see page 92), to serve
pinch of salt	SERVES FOUR

Put the fruit into a buttered ovenproof dish and add caster sugar to taste.

Sift the flour and salt together, toss in the butter or margarine, then rub the fat in until the mixture resembles breadcrumbs. Stir in the Demerara sugar. Spoon the crumble over the fruit and bake at 190°C (375°F) mark 5 for 25–30 minutes until the top is brown and the fruit tender. Serve with custard.

CABINET PUDDING (page 78)

Queen of Puddings

For an extra special finish to this pudding, pipe the meringue in swirls, rosettes, scrolls or a lattice design, then decorate with flaked almonds or chopped pistachio nuts and pieces of glacé or crystallised fruits.
Although not strictly traditional, dried fruits can be added (but omit the rose water) and lemon curd used instead of jam. The rose water in this version adds a medieval touch.

450 ml (¾ pt) milk or a
  mixture of milk and
  cream
40 g (1½ oz) unsalted
  butter, diced
long strip of lemon rind
2 eggs, separated
few drops of rose water
50 g (2 oz) caster sugar
75 g (3 oz) fresh white
  breadcrumbs

about 30 ml (2 tbsp) red
  fruit conserve or good
  quality jam, warmed
flaked almonds or
  chopped pistachio nuts
  and glacé or
  crystallised fruits, to
  decorate

SERVES FOUR

Put the milk, or milk and cream, butter and lemon rind in a saucepan and bring just to simmering point. Stir on to the egg yolks in a bowl, add the rose water and half the sugar, then strain on to the breadcrumbs. Stir the lemon rind back into the mixture. Leave to stand for 20 minutes, then remove the rind.

Pour into a greased 1.1 litre (2 pint) ovenproof dish and bake at 180°C (350°F) mark 4 for about 25 minutes until just set.

Spread the conserve or jam over the pudding. Whisk the egg whites until stiff. Whisk in half the remaining sugar, then gradually whisk in the rest.

Spoon into a piping bag fitted with a star nozzle and pipe decoratively over the pudding. Return to the oven for 15–20 minutes until the meringue is a light golden brown. Decorate with nuts and glacé or crystallised fruits.

Cabinet Pudding

This type of custard-based pudding was very popular in the eighteenth century. Richer versions use single, even double, cream instead of milk, a higher proportion of ratafias, and sometimes brandy is added as well.

425 ml (15 fl oz) milk
vanilla pod
25 g (1 oz) glacé cherries,
  halved
25 g (1 oz) angelica,
  chopped
3 eggs
25 g (1 oz) caster sugar

2 trifle sponge cakes,
  diced
40 g (1½ oz) ratafias,
  crushed
25 g (1 oz) large raisins,
  chopped, or sultanas

SERVES FOUR

Put the milk and the vanilla pod in a saucepan and bring slowly to the boil. Remove from the heat, cover and leave for 15 minutes.

Arrange some of the cherries and angelica in a buttered 750 ml (1¼ pint) plain mould.

Lightly whisk the eggs and sugar together. Remove the vanilla pod from the milk then stir the milk into the eggs.

Mix the sponge cakes, ratafias, raisins or sultanas and remaining cherries and angelica together and spoon into the mould. Strain in the egg and milk and leave to soak for 15 minutes.

Place the mould in a deep baking tin, surround with boiling water and cover with greaseproof paper. Bake at 170°C (325°F) mark 3 for about 1 hour until just set.

Remove the mould from the heat and leave to stand for 2–3 minutes before unmoulding.

Spotted Dick

This is one of the most popular of real English puddings. When well made, Spotted Dick is light and delicious.

75 g (3 oz) fresh white breadcrumbs
75 g (3 oz) self raising flour
pinch of salt
75 g (3 oz) shredded suet
50 g (2 oz) caster sugar
175 g (6 oz) currants

finely grated rind of 1 large lemon
1 egg, beaten
60–90 ml (4–6 tbsp) milk
custard (see page 92), to serve

SERVES FOUR TO SIX

Mix the first seven ingredients together in a bowl, form a well in the centre, add the egg and sufficient milk to give a fairly soft, but not sticky, dough.

Form into a roll on a lightly floured surface, then wrap in greased greaseproof paper. Wrap in foil, securing the seams well, but allowing the pudding plenty of room to rise during cooking. Steam in boiling water for 1½–2 hours, checking the level of the water about every 30 minutes and topping up with more boiling water if necessary.

Serve with custard.

Castle Puddings

This is just one of the many sponge pudding recipes that are such a popular part of traditional English cooking. Folding in whisked egg whites will produce a really feather-light sponge pudding.

100 g (4 oz) unsalted butter, softened
100 g (4 oz) caster sugar
2 eggs, separated
100 g (4 oz) self raising flour
pinch of salt
few drops of vanilla essence

about 45 ml (3 tbsp) blackcurrant, raspberry or strawberry jam
custard (see page 92), to serve

SERVES FOUR

Beat the butter and sugar together in a bowl until light and fluffy. Gradually beat in the egg yolks, then lightly fold in the flour, salt and vanilla essence.

Whisk the egg whites until stiff, but not dry, then lightly fold into the sponge mixture. Divide the jam between eight buttered dariole moulds and divide the sponge mixture between the moulds.

Bake at 180°C (350°F) mark 4 for about 20 minutes until well risen and a light golden colour.

Leave to stand in the moulds for a minute or two before unmoulding on to warmed plates. Serve with custard and extra warmed jam, if liked.

Sussex Pond Pudding

Turn the cooked pudding out on to a warmed plate before serving so that, as it is cut into, the rich, buttery, lemony juices flow out to form a golden pond.

225 g (8 oz) self raising flour	50–75 ml (2–3 fl oz) milk
pinch of salt	about 150 g (5 oz) cold unsalted butter, diced
50 g (2 oz) shredded suet	about 150 g (5 oz) soft light brown sugar
50 g (2 oz) cold butter, coarsely grated	1 large, thin skinned, juicy lemon
5 ml (1 tsp) finely grated lime or lemon rind	
1 egg, beaten	SERVES SIX

Mix the flour and salt together, then stir in the suet, grated butter and lime or lemon rind. Make the egg up to 150 ml (¼ pint) with milk and add to the suet. Quickly mix to a soft, but not sticky, dough.

Knead lightly, then on a lightly floured surface, roll out to a 30 cm (12 inch) round. Cut out one quarter of the dough in a fan shape to within 2.5 cm (1 inch) of the centre and set aside. Use the remaining dough to line a buttered 1.5 litre (2½ pint) pudding basin.

Mix the diced butter and sugar together and place about two thirds in the basin. Prick the lemon well all over with a needle and place on the butter and sugar. Pack the space around the lemon with more butter and sugar, filling the basin completely.

Roll out the reserved dough to a round 2.5 cm (1 inch) larger than the top of the basin. Dampen the exposed edge of the dough lining the basin. Cover with the lid and seal the edges together well.

Cover the top of the basin with a piece of buttered pleated greaseproof paper, then cover with a piece of pleated foil and secure the foil firmly with string.

Put the basin in a large saucepan with enough boiling water to come halfway up the sides of the basin. Cover and steam for 2½ hours, topping up with boiling water as necessary.

Devonshire Whitepot

A delicious light, creamy West Country variation of bread and butter pudding.

3 slices of buttered bread, crusts removed, cut into triangles	finely grated rind of ½ a lemon
600 ml (1 pint) single cream	5 ml (1 tsp) orange flower water
1 egg, beaten	50 g (2 oz) raisins
2 egg yolks	freshly grated nutmeg
50 g (2 oz) caster sugar	SERVES FOUR

Arrange half the bread, buttered side down, in an ovenproof dish. Place the dish in a roasting tin.

Beat the cream, egg, egg yolks, sugar, rind and orange flower water together. Stir in the raisins and pour into the dish. Arrange the remaining bread on top, buttered side uppermost and sprinkle with nutmeg.

Surround the dish with boiling water and bake at 180°C (350°F) mark 4 for about 45 minutes until the pudding is lightly set, and the top crisp and golden.

Bakewell Tart

As with many traditional dishes there are a number of different recipes that are claimed as the genuine, authentic one. In the case of this dish, there is also a dispute about the title of whether it should be called a tart or pudding. The ground almonds in this particularly delicious version can be replaced in part or completely by flour.

shortcrust pastry, made
  with 100 g (4 oz) plain
  flour
50 g (2 oz) unsalted butter
50 g (2 oz) caster sugar
1½ eggs, beaten

100 g (4 oz) ground
  almonds
raspberry jam
icing sugar, for sifting

SERVES FOUR TO SIX

Roll out the pastry on a lightly floured surface and use to line a 15 cm (6 inch) flan ring placed on a baking sheet. Chill for 30 minutes.

Prick the base lightly, cover with greaseproof paper and scatter a layer of baking beans over the paper. Bake blind at 200°C (400°F) mark 6 for 10 minutes. Remove the baking beans and greaseproof lining paper and return the pastry to the oven for a further 5 minutes.

Meanwhile, beat the butter and sugar together in a bowl until light and fluffy, then gradually beat in the eggs, beating well after each addition. Fold in the almonds.

Spread a thin layer of jam over the base of the pastry case. Remove the flan ring and fill the case with the almond mixture. Bake for about 25 minutes until the filling is just firm.

Carefully transfer the cooked tart to a wire rack and sift icing sugar over the top. Serve warm or cold.

Christmas Pudding

This light, moist pudding benefits from 3–4 months maturing.

225 g (8 oz) butter
225 g (8 oz) muscovado
  sugar
3 eggs, beaten
50 g (2 oz) black treacle or
  dark corn syrup
75 g (3 oz) self raising
  flour
pinch of salt
2.5 ml (½ tsp) each of
  ground cinnamon;
  freshly grated nutmeg;
  ground mixed spice

finely grated rind of
  1 orange and 1 lemon
juice of 1 lemon
225 g (8 oz) fresh
  breadcrumbs
225 g (8 oz) each of
  sultanas; raisins;
  currants
50 g (2 oz) mixed peel
50 ml (2 fl oz) brandy
brandy butter (see page
  92), to serve

MAKES TWO 900 G (2 LB) PUDDINGS

Beat the butter until soft, add the sugar and beat until fluffy. Gradually beat in the eggs, then the treacle or syrup.

Sieve the flour, salt and spices together, then fold into the mixture with the fruit rinds, lemon juice, breadcrumbs, fruits, mixed peel and brandy.

Spoon into two 900 g (2 lb) pudding basins. Cover with a circle of greaseproof paper then a piece of aluminium foil, pleated across the centre, and securely tied in place and leave overnight.

Put each basin in a large saucepan with enough water to come halfway up the sides of the basin, cover and steam for 5 hours, then remove from the water. Leave to cool completely then cover with a clean piece of greaseproof paper and a pudding cloth secured with string and the ends of the cloth knotted over the top of the basin. Leave in a cool place. When required, steam for about 3 hours.

Cakes, Buns and Biscuits

T HE CAKES of England are in a class of their own, but the types that are so well-known and loved today did not begin to be made until the eighteenth century. Until then, cakes were really an extension of bread-making, with sugar, spices and dried fruits being added to make a plain yeast dough more interesting.

Modern cake-making evolved as a result of a number of different factors: the use of beaten eggs as a raising agent, the discovery of effective chemical raising agents, such as bicarbonate of soda and cream of tartar, and the construction of enclosed cooking stoves.

Although plain cakes, gingerbreads and rather solid fruit cakes provided fare for country suppers and high teas for years, it was not until the growth of afternoon tea became fashionable amongst the upper classes that cakes developed into the numerous varieties and shapes and sizes that exist nowadays.

Devon Flats

These biscuits are not as rich as a first glance at the list of ingredients may suggest, and they are very easy to make.

225 g (8 oz) self raising
  flour
pinch of salt
100 g (4 oz) caster sugar
100 ml (4 fl oz) clotted
  cream

1 egg, beaten
about 15 ml (1 tbsp) milk,
  to mix

MAKES ABOUT TWENTY-FOUR

Mix the flour and salt together then stir in the sugar. Lightly bind together with the cream, egg and sufficient milk to give a fairly stiff dough. If the dough feels at all sticky, cover it and place in the refrigerator to firm up.

Roll out the dough on a lightly floured surface to about 0.75 cm (⅓ inch) thick and cut into circles with a 7.5 cm (3 inch) cutter. Transfer to a greased baking tray and bake at 220°C (425°F) mark 7 for 8–10 minutes, until a light golden brown. Carefully transfer to a wire rack and leave to cool.

The biscuits can be stored in an airtight container in a cool place for up to 3 days.

Cornish Saffron Cake

Saffron was added to cakes and breads to make them look rich and buttery.

5 ml (1 tsp) caster sugar	5 ml (1 tsp) salt
275 ml (9½ fl oz) warm milk	100 g (4 oz) butter, diced
10 ml (2 tsp) dried yeast	25 g (1 oz) caster sugar
150 ml (¼ pint) boiling water	150 g (5 oz) currants
pinch of saffron strands	100 g (4 oz) chopped mixed peel
450 g (1 lb) strong plain flour	
	MAKES EIGHT SLICES

Grease a 20.5 cm (8 inch) cake tin. Dissolve the sugar in the milk, sprinkle the yeast over the surface and leave in a warm place for 20 minutes until frothy.

Meanwhile, pour the boiling water onto the saffron in a small bowl and leave to infuse.

Sift the flour and salt together. Rub in the butter until the mixture resembles breadcrumbs. Stir in the sugar, currants and peel. Make a well in the centre, strain in the saffron liquid, then add the yeast liquid. Gradually draw the dry ingredients into the liquids and mix to a soft dough.

Put into the prepared tin, cover with a damp cloth and put the tin inside a large polythene bag. Leave until the dough has risen to the top of the tin. This should take about 1 hour in a warm place, 2 hours at room temperature.

Remove from the bag, uncover and bake at 200°C (400°F) mark 6 for 30 minutes. Reduce temperature to 180°C (350°F) mark 4 and bake for 30 minutes.

Leave in the tin for 2–3 minutes before turning out on to a wire rack to cool.

Madeira Cake

The best way to enjoy Madeira cake is with a glass of one of the sweeter Madeiras, as was the custom in the nineteenth century. It can also be served with a cup of coffee at mid-morning or at tea-time.

150 g (5 oz) butter, softened	5 ml (1 tsp) bicarbonate of soda
100 g (4 oz) caster sugar	pinch of salt
4 eggs, beaten	juice of 1 lemon
225 g (8 oz) plain flour	strip of candied citron peel
50 g (2 oz) rice flour or ground rice	
5 ml (1 tsp) cream of tartar	MAKES SIX TO EIGHT SLICES

Grease and base line an 18 cm (7 inch) round cake tin with greaseproof paper.

Cream the butter with the sugar until light and fluffy, then gradually beat in half the egg.

Sift the flour, rice flour or ground rice, cream of tartar, bicarbonate of soda and salt together, then fold into the creamed mixture alternately with the remaining egg and lemon juice.

Turn into the prepared tin and bake at 180°C (350°F) mark 4 for 20 minutes. Open the oven carefully and lay the citron peel on top of the cake. Bake for a further 45 minutes.

Leave to cool in the tin for a few minutes before turning out and leaving to cool, the right way up, on a wire rack.

Muffins

To serve muffins, pull them almost apart through the centre, toast them and spread with butter. Close them up and eat whilst still warm.

5 ml (1 tsp) caster sugar	5 ml (1 tsp) salt
300 ml (½ pint) warm milk	5 ml (1 tsp) plain flour, for dusting
10 ml (2 tsp) dried yeast	5 ml (1 tsp) fine semolina
450 g (1lb) strong plain flour	

MAKES ABOUT FOURTEEN

Dissolve the sugar in the milk, sprinkle the yeast over the surface and leave in a warm place for about 20 minutes until frothy.

Sift the flour and salt together, then form a well in the centre. Pour the yeast liquid into the well, draw in the flour and mix to a smooth dough.

Knead the dough on a lightly floured surface for about 10 minutes until smooth and elastic. Place in a clean bowl, cover with a tea towel and leave in a warm place until doubled in size. Roll out the dough on a lightly floured surface using a lightly floured rolling pin to about 0.5–1 cm (¼–½ inch) thick. Leave to rest, covered, for 5 minutes, then cut into rounds with a 7.5 cm (3 inch) plain cutter.

Place the muffins on a well floured baking sheet. Mix together the flour and semolina and use to dust the tops. Cover with a tea towel and leave in a warm place until doubled in size.

Grease a griddle, electric griddle plate or heavy frying pan and heat over a moderate heat, until a cube of bread turns brown in 20 seconds.

Cook the muffins on the griddle or frying pan for about 7 minutes each side.

Cider Cake

A succulent, moist cake from Somerset, the cider county. Store the cake in an air-tight container for at least 2 days before eating, but it will keep for much longer.

100 g (4 oz) glacé cherries, chopped	1 egg, beaten
100 g (4 oz) currants	175 g (6 oz) plain flour
100 g (4 oz) sultanas	25 g (1 oz) cornflour
100 g (4 oz) raisins	10 ml (2 tsp) baking powder
150 ml (¼ pint) dry cider	pinch of salt
150 g (5 oz) light soft brown sugar	

MAKES EIGHT TO TEN SLICES

Put the fruit and the cider in a bowl and leave to soak in a cool place overnight.

Stir in the sugar and egg, then sift in the flour, cornflour, baking powder and salt. Mix well together, then transfer to a greased 900 g (2 lb) loaf tin. Bake at 170°C (325°F) mark 3 for 2 hours.

Leave to cool slightly in the tin, then turn out on to a wire rack and leave to cool.

MUFFINS (above)

Crumpets

Serve the crumpets toasted, preferably in front of an open fire, with butter, or cheese as well, or try them as a base for poached or scrambled eggs.

5 ml (1 tsp) caster sugar	5 ml (1 tsp) salt
750 ml (1¼ pints) warm milk	2.5 ml (½ tsp) bicarbonate of soda
10 ml (2 tsp) dried yeast	
450 g (1 lb) plain flour	MAKES ABOUT FIFTEEN

Dissolve the sugar in 300 ml (½ pint) of the milk, sprinkle the yeast over the surface then leave in a warm place for about 10 minutes until frothy.

Sift the flour and salt into a warm bowl and form a well in the centre. Pour half the yeast liquid into the well, then gradually draw the flour into the liquid using a wooden spoon and beat until smooth. Gradually beat in the remaining liquid to give a thin, smooth batter.

Beat well, then cover with a clean tea towel and leave in a warm place until the mixture has doubled in size.

Dissolve the bicarbonate of soda in the remaining milk, beat it into the batter well, then leave for 30 minutes.

Grease a griddle, electric griddle plate or heavy frying pan and three 9 cm (3½ inch) plain metal cutters or crumpet rings.

Heat the griddle or pan and the rings over a moderate heat until a cube of bread turns brown in 20 seconds. Pour enough batter into each ring to fill them to a depth of about 1 cm (½ inch).

Cook for about 4 minutes until the surface is dry and honeycombed with holes. Carefully remove the rings and turn the crumpets over and cook on the other side for 2–3 minutes. Continue until all the batter is used, greasing and heating the griddle and rings before adding the batter.

Parkin

English parkin recipes originate in the north of the country and always contain oatmeal, syrup and black treacle. They keep well and should be left for 2 or 3 days in an air-tight container before being eaten.

175 g (6 oz) golden syrup	2.5 ml (½ tsp) ground cinnamon
175 g (6 oz) black treacle	
50 g (2 oz) lard, diced	7.5 ml (1½ tsp) bicarbonate of soda
50 g (2 oz) butter or margarine, diced	
	225 g (8 oz) medium oatmeal
100 g (4 oz) soft brown sugar	
	1 egg, lightly beaten
225 g (8 oz) plain flour	60 ml (4 tbsp) milk
pinch of salt	
10 ml (2 tsp) ground ginger	MAKES TWELVE SLICES

Grease and line a 23 cm (9 inch) square tin.

Gently warm the syrup and treacle, lard, butter or margarine and sugar together in a small saucepan until the treacle and fats have melted and the sugar has dissolved.

Sift the flour, salt, spices and bicarbonate of soda together in a bowl and stir in the oatmeal. Form a well in the centre, then add the egg and milk, beaten together.

Pour the warm ingredients into the milk, then gradually draw the dry ingredients into the liquid mixture and beat well to give a smooth batter.

Pour into the prepared tin and bake at 180°C (350°F) mark 4 for about 1 hour.

Allow to stand for about 2 minutes before turning out on to a wire rack. Leave for 2 minutes then carefully remove the lining paper. Turn the cake the right way up and leave to cool.

Store in an airtight tin for 2–3 days before eating.

Chelsea Buns

Yeast fruit buns were a speciality of the old Chelsea Bun House, Grosvenor Row, and are said to have been bought by, or for, King Georges II, III and IV. Serve freshly made and warm.

225 g (8 oz) strong plain flour	25 g (1 oz) mixed peel, chopped
7.5 ml (1½ tsp) dried yeast	50 g (2 oz) soft brown sugar
5 ml (1 tsp) caster sugar	40 g (1½ oz) butter, melted
100 ml (4 fl oz) warm milk	icing sugar, for glazing
2.5 ml (½ tsp) salt	
25 g (1 oz) butter, diced	
1 egg, beaten	MAKES TWELVE
75 g (3 oz) sultanas, currants and chopped raisins, mixed	

Grease an 18–20.5 cm (7–8 inch) square tin.

Sift 50 g (2 oz) of the flour into a warm bowl. Stir in the yeast. Dissolve the caster sugar in the milk and stir into the flour and yeast. Leave in a warm

place for about 20 minutes until frothy.

Sift the remaining flour and salt into a warm bowl, then rub in the diced butter. Form a well in the centre, pour in the yeast mixture and the egg, then draw in the dry ingredients to make a smooth dough. Knead for 10 minutes.

Place the dough in a clean bowl, cover with a clean tea towel and leave to rise for 1¼–2¼ hours until doubled in size. Knead the dough lightly on a floured surface, then roll it out to a large rectangle, about 30×23 cm (12×9 inches).

Mix the dried fruit, peel and sugar together. Brush the dough with melted butter, then scatter the fruit mixture over the surface, leaving a 2.5 cm (1 inch) clear border around the edges.

Roll the dough up tightly like a Swiss roll, starting at a long edge. Press the edges together to seal them. Cut the roll into 12 slices.

Place the rolls cut side uppermost in the prepared tin. Cover with a clean tea towel and leave in a warm place until doubled in size.

Bake at 190°C (350°F) mark 5 for 30 minutes. Blend a little icing sugar with water to make a sugar glaze and brush over the top while still hot. Leave to cool slightly in the tin before turning out.

Carrot Cake

The flavour improves if the cake is kept for a few days before adding the topping.

225 g (8 oz) butter or margarine, diced
225 g (8 oz) light soft brown sugar
4 eggs, separated
10 ml (2 tsp) grated orange rind
15 ml (1 tbsp) lemon juice
175 g (6 oz) self raising flour
5 ml (1 tsp) baking powder
50 g (2 oz) ground almonds

100 g (4 oz) chopped walnuts
350 g (12 oz) young carrots, grated

Topping (optional)
200 g (7 oz) soft cheese
10 ml (2 tsp) clear honey
5 ml (1 tsp) lemon juice
25 g (1 oz) chopped walnuts

MAKES EIGHT SLICES

Grease and line a 20.5 cm (8 inch) round cake tin.

Beat the butter or margarine and sugar together in a bowl until light and fluffy. Beat in the egg yolks, then stir in the orange rind and lemon juice.

Sift the flour and baking powder, then stir into the mixture with the ground almonds and the walnuts.

Whisk the egg whites until stiff and fold into the cake mixture with the carrots. Pour into the prepared tin and hollow the centre slightly. Bake at 180°C (350°F) mark 4 for about 1½ hours, covering the top with foil after an hour if it starts to brown.

Leave to cool slightly, then turn out on to a wire rack and remove the lining paper. Leave to cool.

Beat the cheese, honey and lemon juice and spread over the cake. Sprinkle with walnuts.

Eccles Cakes

These crisp, plump, buttery pastries were once considered to be so sinfully rich that they were banned. They are named after the Lancashire town of Eccles. Serve them, still warm, as a tea-time treat.

puff pastry, made using 225 g (8 oz) flour
40 g (1½ oz) caster sugar
2.5 ml (½ tsp) ground mixed spice
100 g (4 oz) currants
40 g (1½ oz) chopped mixed peel

25 g (1 oz) butter, melted
lightly beaten egg white and granulated sugar, for glazing

MAKES SIXTEEN TO TWENTY

Roll out the pastry to 0.3 cm (⅛ inch) thickness on a lightly floured surface using a floured rolling pin. Cut into circles using a 10 cm (4 inch) plain cutter.

Mix the sugar and spice together, then stir in the currants, peel and butter. Place 5 ml (1 tsp) of the fruit mixture on the centre of each circle. Brush the edges with beaten egg white, then draw them up over the filling and pinch them together to seal. Turn the pastries over and roll lightly to flatten them slightly. Cut three parallel slits in the top of each, brush with egg white and sprinkle with sugar.

Place on a dampened baking sheet, and bake at 220°C (425°F) mark 7 for about 15 minutes until golden brown.

Transfer to a wire rack to cool slightly before serving.

BRANDY SNAPS (page 90), CARROT CAKE (above)
AND ECCLES CAKES (above)

Brandy Snaps

Brandy snaps were popular as Fairings – that is they used to be sold, or given as gifts, at country fairs. They can be kept, unfilled, in an airtight container for up to a week.

50 g (2 oz) butter, cubed
50 g (2 oz) caster sugar
30 ml (2 tbsp) golden
  syrup
50 g (2 oz) plain flour
2.5 ml (½ tsp) ground
  ginger
5 ml (1 tsp) brandy

finely grated rind of ½ a
  lemon

Filling
175 ml (6 fl oz) double
  cream

MAKES ABOUT TWELVE

Line two or three large baking sheets with non-stick baking paper.

Gently heat the butter, sugar and syrup until the butter has melted and the sugar dissolved. Remove from the heat.

Sift the flour and ginger together, then stir into the melted mixture with the brandy and lemon rind.

Drop teaspoonfuls of the mixture on to a prepared baking sheet, leaving about 10 cm (4 inches) in between them. Bake towards the hottest part of the oven at 180°C (350°F) mark 4 for about 7 minutes until the biscuits are bubbling and lacy in appearance.

Meanwhile, prepare another tray of the mixture ready for baking. As soon as the baked biscuits are cooked, remove them from the baking sheet using a palette knife and roll each one around the buttered handle of a wooden spoon. Leave on the handles until set, then gently twist each one, remove it and leave to cool completely.

If the biscuits set before they have been shaped, return them to the oven for a few minutes to soften. Store in an airtight container until required.

Just before serving, whip the cream until it stands in soft peaks. Spoon into a piping bag fitted with a star nozzle and pipe the cream into the snaps.

Dorset Apple Cake

This simple, delicious version of apple cake comes from Dorset and is at its best if served still warm, with custard or brandy butter (see page 92) for a pudding, or plain butter for tea or with mid-morning coffee.

225 g (8 oz) plain flour
7.5 ml (1½ tsp) baking
  powder
pinch of salt
100 g (4 oz) butter, diced
165 g (5½ oz) soft light
  brown sugar

175 g (6 oz) peeled and
  cored cooking apple,
  chopped
1 egg, beaten
milk, to mix
2.5 ml (½ tsp) ground
  cinnamon

MAKES SIX TO EIGHT SLICES

Grease and line an 18 cm (7 inch) round cake tin.

Sift the flour, baking powder and salt together. Rub in the butter until mixture resembles crumbs.

Stir in 100 g (4 oz) of the sugar, the apple and the egg. Mix to a dough adding a little milk if too stiff.

Put into the prepared tin. Mix the remaining sugar with the cinnamon and sprinkle over the top. Bake at 180°C (350°F) mark 4 for about 45–50 minutes until a light golden brown and cooked through.

Cool in the tin for 12 minutes, then turn out.

Lardy Cake

Recipes for this traditional tea-time cake originate from several counties, particularly Wiltshire, Oxfordshire and Cambridgeshire. Serve it freshly baked, warm and upside down on a warm plate, and break, don't cut the cake, into pieces.

5 ml (1 tsp) caster sugar	175 g (6 oz) mixed
300 ml (½ pint) warm	sultanas and currants
water	50 g (2 oz) chopped mixed
10 ml (2 tsp) dried yeast	peel
450 g (1 lb) strong plain	175 g (6 oz) granulated
flour	sugar
10 ml (2 tsp) salt	
175 g (6 oz) hard lard	MAKES EIGHT SLICES

Grease a 20.5×25 cm (8×10 inch) tin. Dissolve the sugar in the water, sprinkle the yeast over the surface then leave in a warm place for about 20 minutes until frothy.

Sift the flour and salt together into a bowl. Dice 15 g (½ oz) of the lard, toss in the flour, then rub it in. Form a well in the centre, pour in the yeast liquid, then draw in the dry ingredients and mix to a dough that leaves the sides of the bowl clean.

Turn on to a lightly floured work surface and knead well for 10 minutes until smooth and elastic. Place in a clean bowl. Cover with a damp cloth, put the bowl inside a large polythene bag and leave until doubled in size. This will take about 1 hour in a warm room, about 2 hours at normal room temperature.

Turn the dough on to a floured surface and roll out to a rectangle about 0.5 cm (¼ inch) thick. Cut the remaining lard into small pieces and dot one third of it over the surface of the dough and sprinkle over one third of the fruit, peel and sugar. Fold the dough in three, folding the bottom third up and the top third down. Give a half turn, then repeat the process twice more.

Roll the dough out to fit the prepared tin. Cover with oiled polythene and a cloth and leave to rise in a warm place for 20–30 minutes until puffy. Score the top into eight rectangles, then bake at 220°C (425°F) mark 7 for about 45 minutes.

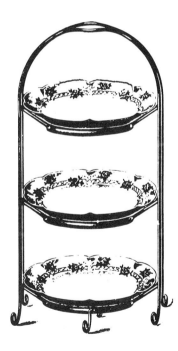

Traditional Accompaniments

OVER THE years, combinations of ideal accompaniments to complement a main dish have evolved. Some accompaniments are fairly specific, such as Yorkshire pudding to serve with roast beef. Others, such as redcurrant jelly, will enhance a number of different dishes.

Brandy Butter

Serve brandy butter with Christmas pudding, mince pies or with hot fruit or spicy desserts.

225 g (8 oz) unsalted butter, diced	75 ml (3 fl oz) cognac or other good brandy
100 g (4 oz) icing sugar	squeeze of lemon juice

Beat the butter in a slightly warmed bowl until it is smooth and light. Gradually beat in the icing sugar. When most of it has been incorporated, start to gradually add the brandy, alternating with the remaining sugar, and beat until the sauce is light and fluffy. Beat in the lemon juice.

Pile into a cold bowl, cover and leave in a cold place to allow the flavours to mature before serving.

Custard

This is traditional English custard which can be served hot, warm or cold with all manner of puddings. If it is to be served cold, cover the surface closely with clingfilm to prevent a skin forming.

600 ml (1 pint) milk or mixture of milk and cream	4 egg yolks, beaten
1 vanilla pod	MAKES 600 ML (1 PINT)
about 30 ml (2 tbsp) caster sugar	

Gently heat the milk, or milk and cream, with the vanilla pod to just below simmering point. Cover, remove from the heat and leave to infuse for 15 minutes. Remove the vanilla pod.

Blend the sugar and egg yolks, then gradually stir in the milk, or milk and cream. Pour into a clean saucepan and heat gently, stirring, until the sauce thickens enough to coat the back of the spoon. Do not allow to boil.

Redcurrant Jelly

Redcurrant jelly can be served with any lamb, game or even chicken dishes.

1.5 kg (3 lb) redcurrants
600 ml (1 pint) water
sugar

Place the currants in a preserving pan with the water and simmer gently for about 30 minutes until the fruit is very tender.

Spoon the fruit into a scalded jelly bag or treble thickness of muslin or cheesecloth attached to the legs of an upturned stool, and leave to strain into a clean bowl. Leave to drip naturally without squeezing the bag or cloth as this would make the jelly cloudy.

Measure the liquid, pour it back into the pan and add 450 g (1 lb) sugar for each 600 ml (1 pint) liquid. Heat gently, stirring with a wooden spoon, until the sugar has dissolved. Bring to the boil and boil rapidly for 10–15 minutes or until the setting point is reached.

To test for setting point, drop a tiny amount of the jelly on to a cold saucer, leave to cool, then push the jelly with a finger. If the surface of the jelly wrinkles, the setting point has been reached. Remove the pan from the heat while carrying out the test.

Pour into warmed, sterilised jars, and put waxed discs, wax side down, on the surface of the jelly. Cover immediately with a dampened round of cellophane. Store in a cool place.

Bread Sauce

This is the traditional accompaniment to roast chicken, turkey and game.

350 ml (12 fl oz) milk
½ an onion, stuck with
  2 cloves
½ bay leaf
3 black peppercorns
1 blade of mace
90 ml (6 tbsp) fresh white
  breadcrumbs

salt
15 g (½ oz) butter
about 30 ml (2 tbsp)
  cream (optional)

SERVES FOUR

Bring the milk to the boil with the onion stuck with cloves, the ½ bay leaf, peppercorns and mace. Remove from the heat, cover and leave to infuse for 30 minutes.

Strain the milk, then bring to simmering point. Gradually stir in the breadcrumbs, then simmer for 3 minutes, stirring. Season and stir in the butter and cream, if using. Serve as soon as possible.

Cumberland Sauce

Cumberland sauce is served cold as a traditional accompaniment to all manner of game dishes, both hot and cold. It will keep for several weeks if stored in a covered glass jar in the refrigerator.

1 large lemon
1 large orange
150 ml (¼ pint) water
225 g (8 oz) redcurrant
  jelly
5 ml (1 tsp) Dijon
  mustard

salt and pepper
sprinkling of ground
  ginger
75 ml (3 fl oz) tawny port

Thinly pare the rind from the orange and lemon, avoiding the pith, using a potato peeler.

Cut the rind into very fine strips, then place in a small saucepan with the water. Bring to the boil and simmer for 5 minutes. Drain and refresh under cold running water.

Squeeze the juice from the fruit and strain into a bowl. Stir in the jelly, mustard and seasoning and place the bowl over a saucepan of hot water and heat, stirring, until the jelly has melted. Stir in the port and fruit rinds and continue to heat until the sauce begins to thicken.

Pour into a dish or into a glass jar if the sauce is to be kept.

Index